Meghan,

May this be a
season of victory
after victory!

# Endorsements

I have enjoyed working with Jermaine side by side in ministry for more than 10 years. During that time I have witnessed the Man of God that Jermaine has demonstrated. Faithfulness and fortitude are two of the strong qualities which are regular fruit in his Christian walk. This book is a testament to the life of overcoming success I have seen Jermaine live. I look forward to continued pleasure as I watch his life of Victory in Jesus!

**Prophet Bill Lackie**
**Frontline International**

Perhaps the most humbling task we have as Christians is to receive the victory that Jesus has won for us. Sometimes we struggle in defeat because we don't know what we have access to. I eagerly await people being impacted by this book…it's needed.

**Darrell D. Patrick**
**Darrell Patrick Ministries, Inc.**

I have been thoroughly edified by every page of Break up with Defeat. Jermaine does a meticulous yet practical job of exposing the characteristics of defeatism, highlighting potential, and lifting the reader to a place of ascertaining victory in their personal lives. I will definitely be purchasing a copy for each of the leaders that surround me in my company and church. They will only be provoked for the better as have I, and you, if you pick up this book today.

**Dwayne Howard**
**Chief Steward of Kainos Creative Studios, Elder at New Dimensions Ministries, Co-Founder of Awake The Flame, and Author of Leader Ecology**

Far too often, the world wants us to believe that life is a zero-sum game; that it's simply about winning or losing. In "Break up with Defeat" Jermaine unlocks the truth about real victory. He reveals the beauty and power of living a life of true Victory.

**Jason Catalano**
**School Board Member District 5 Walton County, FL**

Jermaine Francis communicators in a real way the truth about victory. This book will connect with your heart and bring you fresh hope. It will also challenge and encourage you.

**Shannon E. Young,**
**Worship Director at Kingdom Life Fellowship, Sewell, New Jersey**

Have you ever said, "there is more to my life than this?" Break up with Defeat is a must-have resource in your arsenal filled with real life accounts and strategies on living a victorious life. Jermaine Francis has been graced by God to awaken a generation of forerunners and world shakers.

**Torrey Marcel Harper**
**Director of Times Square House of Prayer, NYC**

I was so excited to pick up the 1st book by Jermaine Francis on victory and get a behind the scenes glimpse into his life. Over the last 15 years he's lived a life of victory which is evident in his book and during the last 10 years he's spent at Christian International he got to see victory in action by a ministry that has operated in victory for over 50 years and the lives of countless individuals who've lived out the principles in his book.

**Andre walker**
**Founder of Hydro**

# Break Up with Defeat

Recognize and Shatter Hidden
Mindsets That Defeat You

JERMAINE FRANCIS

WESTBOW
PRESS®
A DIVISION OF THOMAS NELSON
& ZONDERVAN

WestBow Press books may be ordered through booksellers or by contacting:

WestBow Press
A Division of Thomas Nelson & Zondervan
1663 Liberty Drive
Bloomington, IN 47403
www.westbowpress.com
1 (866) 928-1240

ISBN: 978-1-5127-7233-3 (sc)
ISBN: 978-1-5127-7234-0 (hc)
ISBN: 978-1-5127-7232-6 (e)

Library of Congress Control Number: 2017900793

Print information available on the last page.

WestBow Press rev. date: 2/14/2017

# Contents

# DEDICATION

*To my mom Marlene Rose, who made sure I
had a Godly foundation in my life.*

*To my grandmother Gloria March, who gave
all she could to see me succeed.*

# Foreword

## BY JANE HAMON

> Dear friends, I've dropped everything to write you
> about this life of salvation that we have in common. I
> have to write insisting—begging!—that you fight with
> everything you have in you for this faith entrusted to
> us as a gift to guard and cherish. Jude 1:3 The Message

I have often said to our congregation, "I am more afraid of my SELF than
I am of the devil." While I recognize our spiritual enemy has certain dark
power, I also recognize the truth of God's Word that "Greater is He that
is in me than he that is in the world." Christ in me is greater than any
spiritual force the devil can throw against me.

So then why do we as Believers struggle to live the life of an
Overcomer? One reason is that in order to be an Overcomer, by
definition, one must have things to overcome. We all love the idea of
victory, however, in truth, there is no victory without a battle. This
is not necessarily a message most Believers want to hear, but one that
when faced will empower us to confront whatever difficulties arise to
challenge our peace.

As a young woman in ministry I was quite bold in stepping out to
use my spiritual gifts. I wasn't afraid to be in front of people. I wasn't
afraid of letting my voice be heard. Yet I had a stronghold of fear in my
life that others were not aware of. It was unreasonable but it was very
real. I struggled with a "spirit" of fear which would paralyze me in the
middle of the night. I eventually had a breakthrough of deliverance from
the demonic influence that was holding me captive, however, I then had

to wage a war in my mind in order to stay free. I had to learn to take captive every thought, every vain imagination and every mindset that would set me up for defeat.

Life is a battle and this earth is our battlefield. When Paul tells us in Ephesians 6 that we need to put on the whole armor of God he begins by having us put on the helmet of salvation. Why? Because he knew that to successfully and strategically navigate this battlefield we would need to have our minds and hearts in full alignment and agreement with the Word of God and our identity in Christ. We must get our SELF in line for it is our own mind that will set us up for defeat. Paul knew that true victory did not depend on having peace in our outward circumstances but rather that by having peace and strength in our inward man we can actually experience triumph in every trial.

This is one of the reasons I am so excited about this book. Breakup with Defeat will inspire you to break free of limitations and live a life of freedom as God intended from your birth. It will take you from feeling like a victim to realizing you are actually a victor in life. It provides the reader with powerful insights and tools which will empower you to overcome a life of defeat and fatalism and instead live a life full of celebrating one victory after another.

The other reason I am so excited about this book is that it is written by one of my spiritual sons, and one of my favorite people, Jermaine Francis. I have watched him grow into a powerful prophetic voice, an anointed preacher and a cutting edge example to the generations. But more than that, he is a good husband to his wife Rebecca (also one of my favorite people), a loyal friend and a man of faith and transparency. He is a man who has not just written a book from theory, but has drawn on his own journey of learning to walk in victory as an Overcomer in Christ. He will inspire you to do the same as you realize you can Breakup with Defeat!

Apostle Jane Hamon
Vision Church @ Christian International
Author of *Dreams and Visions*, *The Deborah Company* and *The Cyrus Decree*

# Introduction

Are you in a relationship with defeat? Hmmm, you just might be. Let's check to see. Do you feel drained, overwhelmed, tired, unmotivated, or empty? Do you feel like you're just going through the motions, like things seem like they will never change, like the joy is gone, or like you're always looking ahead to something more exciting? If so, you could be in a relationship to defeat.

During my last year of elementary school, about three weeks before school ended, the teacher called me to her desk. I knew for sure I was in trouble for something. She told me I had to go meet another teacher in the administration offices. I had no idea what was going on. I did not even know who this other teacher was. I figured I was in trouble for something, but I just did not know what. I thought I must have done something bad that I forgot about. So I went to meet the other teacher, and when I got to her office, there was another girl there. The teacher sat us down and gave us both a folder with a lot of paper in it. She said, "I want you to read these papers out loud to me." I thought, "I guess I must be having problems reading, so now we must have to do extra work." I thought "Man, life is so hard. This is going to cut in to my TV watching time. O the injustice." I read the paper out loud to her, shy and timid, and I had a hard time with some of the words. The teacher then told us we would be meeting a few times a week to go over this paper. I felt unsure of myself. I did not know what this was all about. At the end of the meeting, she explained, "You guys have been chosen out of the graduating student body to be master of ceremony at graduation." I had the opportunity to present awards to leaders in the community and to introduce local government officials. I thought in my head, "What an honor! That's cool, but come on lady, you could have led with that. I was over here having a panic attack. I was making new career goals of cleaning car windows at the stop lights at the busiest intersections." I was a little dramatic in my head.

My confidence changed once I understood the honor I was given. I had thought I was in trouble. I did not know I was chosen to do something special and honorable. They waited until the end to tell me that part. They wanted to see me sweat I guess.

We often act like what we believe about ourselves. Once I understood the privilege I was given, I then had more confidence. On graduation day, I was loud and proud as I read the order of service. I presented awards to local community leaders with confidence. It was an exciting day. I felt like the king of the world, or at least king of my world.

I believe many Christians feel lost and unsure of themselves just like I did as a little boy. So many believers are need breakthrough in so many areas of their lives on a consistent basis. Why are so many still struggling?

I believe many of us are still struggling because we have believed the enemy's lie about ourselves. That lie may be one of the most paralyzingly lies there is. It leaves you feeling lost, empty, rejected, abandoned, and worthless. "What is the lie," you may ask? The lie is that you are defeated. When we believe we are defeated, we are in a relationship with defeat. You may say, "I don't believe that lie." It may prove truer than you realize when you examine the evidence in your life, especially the way you react to hard things. The enemy wants us to believe we are defeated. God wants us to know we have been chosen for victory. In this book, I will lead you on a journey to break up with defeat.

# one

## WHAT IS VICTORY?

As believers we often hear the terms, "We have the victory," "I have read the back of the book, and we win," "Victory is ours," or "Shout for the victory." These things have truth to them. It sounds exciting. I don't think God is just out to excite us though. I think he is out to transform us. We often clap and cheer without knowing what that means or what to actually do with it. We made some noise. We may feel a little better.

When the service ends, we pick up our stuff and head out the building to face the same problems we walked in with. We still have areas in life that we can clearly look at and say that victory is definitely not present there, even after we clapped and cheered. Are we doing something wrong? Not necessarily. But could we be missing something? We all believe deep down that God has more for us than many of us are experiencing. At least I hope you believe that.

I want to help move you from just being excited about victory. I want this concept of victory that's floating around out there to become alive in you. I want you to move into a life of victory. I want you to become a living example of victory. To begin the journey to victory, we must first build a foundation. Let's start with defining victory.

> vic·to·ry [vik-tuh-ree, vik-tree]
> noun, plural vic·to·ries.
> 1. a success or triumph over an enemy in battle or war.
> 2. an engagement ending in such triumph: American victories in the Pacific were won at great cost.

3. the ultimate and decisive superiority in any battle or contest: The new vaccine effected a victory over poliomyelitis.
4. a success or superior position achieved against any opponent, opposition, difficulty, etc.: a moral victory.[1]

The definition above shows that victory has to do with your position over an opponent. Victory is positional.

## WE ALL LOVE VICTORY

When a sports team has a victory, the assumption is that a loser is present. You can't have victory without an opposition to triumph over. There is only one question asked when someone returns from a sporting event. The million-dollar question is "Who won?" Why is this the first question asked? We want to know who got the victory. We don't ask who lost. We are less interested in the defeated party.

We all love victory. We all love victors. That's why we watch sports, hoping for our favorite team to win. We cheer and yell at the TV, hoping we can help our team achieve victory. We watch from our living rooms miles away from the stadium. We're possibly wearing a jersey or memorabilia from our favorite team. We desire to contribute to that victory. In my mind, I am out there playing with the team.

I love watching track and field in the Olympics. It is in my blood, having a Jamaican heritage. When I'm watching, I stand up and run in place. I move my hands back and forth as fast as I can. I really do believe it helps them run faster. I am brought back to reality when my wife says to take out the trash because it's stinking up the house. That then reminds me I am in my living room.

For the same reasons, we love superhero movies. The hero has to fight his way through one hundred obstacles. The hero overcomes them all to now face the main bad guy. He fights courageously and defeats the bad guy. We want to feel like we have come out victorious against whatever obstacle was in front of us. We desire to know we can see a challenge and rise to meet that challenge. Our hearts say we want to do what looks like cannot be done. We want to have victory over our opponent.

## VICTORY IS NOISY

My wife and I were at Rockefeller Center in New York City during a presidential election night one year. There were hundreds of people gathered. They were showing the results state by state on a big screen as they came in. All the news outlets were there. As the results came in, you could see who was leading in electoral votes. At this point, you were pretty sure who won. Then they made the official announcement about who won. The crowd erupted with cheers and howls, like one mass unit, with a deafening noise. It was a little intimidating to stand there and watch this happen. Then we decided we should start heading back to where we were staying to beat the crowd. We made our way out of the crowd, and for several blocks away, we could still hear them cheering as one voice. It sounded like a roar.

The same thing happens when a sports team wins a championship. The fans in the crowd shout, high five, chest bump, and scream as loud as they can. There is a burst of energy that shoots through that room. It can't be ignored or overlooked. It is in your face, and it is making itself known. You can't even hear the person next to you. The cheers can echo outside of the building. Why? Because victory is present, and victory is noisy. Victory is self-announcing.

Have you ever watched the game shows where winners get a car or a dream vacation? You notice that you don't get a golf clap or a polite smile and thank you. The winners usually run and jump and shout. There is life, there is movement, there is noise. They can't be held back. They know they have achieved it and have received what they have been fighting for. All of their hard work has produced something tangible. They have victory.

## VICTORY IS TEMPORARY

What is the standard for victory? Do you have victory when you win one game? Or is it when you win the championship? If you win the championship of a sporting event this year, what happens next year? How many losses make you no longer a victor?

Teams that win a championship in any sport have a mark in history. They will be remembered as the team that won the championship in a specific year. Sports commentators will often put contingencies on why they won. They won because the other team was injured, tired, etc. A team may be able to win many championships, year after year. At the same time, they can't keep that up forever. They will lose a game, or someone will have to retire, at some point. Someone will come along and break their record. They can't stay on top forever.

The natural standards of victory are temporary. You will not be known as a victor by this world's standard forever. Nations rise and fall. Armies are defeated. Champions are on top now, but it will not last forever. Someone or something will come along that is stronger, faster, smarter, younger, or more technologically advanced. It's only a matter of time. All human efforts of victory have an expiration date.

These have all been examples of natural victory. There is another realm of victory though. There is only one place in existence that you can be in the state of victory forever. Wait for it … that is in the kingdom of God. You can enter the state of victorious living every day with the Victorious One.

--------

[1] "Victory." Dictionary.com. Accessed November 10, 2015. http://www.dictionary.com/browse/victory?s=t.

# two

## DEFEAT

We took a look at victory and got an understanding of it. Before we continue in the things of victory, let's look at the enemy of victory, which is defeat. I want to show you what defeat looks like, and I would like to discuss its characteristics. Let's start with defining the word.

> de.feat
> 1. to overcome in a contest, election, battle, etc.; prevail over; vanquish: They defeated the enemy. She defeated her brother at tennis.
> 2. to frustrate; thwart.
> 3. to eliminate or deprive of something expected: The early returns defeated his hopes of election.[2]

Defeat is the process of being overcome in some kind of battle, sporting match, or challenge. It means you did not succeed in achieving a certain goal with set boundaries. So the goal in war may be to kill the enemy before the enemy kills you. In sports, the goal is scoring more points than an opposing team. In business, the goal is making enough money for your business to stay open and to pay yourself and your employees. Whatever the challenge may be, not being able to achieve it is defeat.

## DEFEATISM

Consistently not being able to achieve a set goal can be discouraging. For example, you keep trying to lose weight or to get out of debt, but you can't. A mindset of defeat starts to settle in. This is called defeatism.

> Defeatism is acceptance of defeat without struggle. In everyday use, defeatism has a negative connotation and is often linked to pessimism in psychology. The term is commonly used in the politics and especially in the context of war to denote treason: a soldier can be a defeatist if he or she refuses to fight because he or she thinks that the fight will be lost for sure or that it is not worth fighting for some other reason. Again in connection with war, the term is used to refer to the view that defeat would be better than victory. The term can also be used in other fields, like politics, sport, psychology and philosophy.[3]

With defeatism, you feel like you cannot succeed or win. It's carrying an internal heavy weight. The simplest task seems impossible. You have already lost before you start. More excuses arise than reasons to overcome. You feel like no one understands how hard it is for you to accomplish certain goals. You feel like you have no energy to fight. You feel like a mouse against a dinosaur. You can't even think clearly of how to overcome. You see no way out of your situation. Defeat does not fight fair. It will leave you stripped of confidence and render you paralyzed.

## HOW DEFEAT WORKS

A defeated heart leaves you dry and with a crushed spirit.

> A cheerful disposition is good for your health; gloom and doom leave you bone-tired. (Proverbs 17:22 MSG)

> A cheerful heart is good medicine, but a crushed spirit dries up the bones. (Proverbs 17:22 NIV)

Giving up is the doorway of giving in to defeat. Once you give up in your heart, you will now see things through the eyes of defeat. Everything will look unattainable. Your mind will help reinforce your heart's feelings. It becomes a factory producing the best and most convincing excuses possible. It will cause you to look at people who are accomplishing what you want with reasons that disqualify you.

You will see other people's actions as bad. You see others succeeding as a negative thing. You believe they are taking advantage of people: "They come from money," or "They are people pleasers." Whatever the excuse is, it makes you feel better about yourself, giving you a false noble feeling. There could be one million excuses why you feel this way, but at the core, defeat is in operation. Defeat deflates. It takes the breath of hope out of life.

I recently heard an interview with a popular minister. He was asked why he always talks so positively in all of his messages. He said, "Most people have been beaten up by life so much that I am just trying to give them some place to hear God's hope." That is a good point. He has a large church. The masses are looking for that hope. I think it is great to share and minister on God's hope. However, people have to be equipped to learn to live out this hope by the power of the Holy Spirit. If not, what I see happen to many people is that attending church becomes almost equal to a drug. It gives them hope for a few days at most, and then they shrink back into the defeat that is dominating their lives. It is a quick fix but does not break the defeat off their souls. I will show how to live out this hope in later chapters.

## THE ORIGIN OF DEFEAT

> And the God of peace shall bruise Satan under your feet
> shortly. The grace of our Lord Jesus Christ be with you.
> Amen. (Romans 16:20 KJV)

From this scripture we see Satan's position. It is under the feet, a place of lowness and defeat. Satan's posture is one of inferiority. Let's look at another scripture that describes Satan's position.

> Instead, you will be brought down to the place of the dead,
> down to its lowest depths.
> Everyone there will stare at you and ask,
> 'Can this be the one who shook the earth

7

and made the kingdoms of the world tremble?
Is this the one who destroyed the world
and made it into a wasteland?
Is this the king who demolished the world's greatest cities
and had no mercy on his prisoners?"
(Isaiah 14:15-17 NTL)

The Lord shows us that Satan is weak and unimpressive. He has no real authority or power; he only seduces us into giving up ours.

In Genesis 3 :1-7 (NIV) Satan approaches Eve. He convinces her that if she eats of the tree that God has instructed them not to eat, that they would be like God. However, in Genesis 1:27 (NIV) it said that God had already made them in His likeness and image. The serpent offered Eve something she already had. The enemy has no power or authority over us. He only lies to us so that we will give up our authority to him. The enemy gained authority in Adam and Eve's lives by convincing them to believe what he said over what God said. The enemy can only occupy the places that we have given up. The enemy tries to cause us to give up our God-given authority. In exchange, he gives us the only thing he has to offer, defeat.

Satan seeks to get his poison into us and make us carriers of his defeat. If you have been operating in defeat, you are in the enemy's territory.

## SHAKE OFF DEFEAT

In Bible college, I had a great opportunity to be a part of the traveling dance/ drama team. I only joined to be a part of the drama team. However, to be a part of the drama team, you also had to join the dance team, because it was one group that did both. You had to try out to be on the team. It was only because God wanted me on the team that I made it through tryouts, I am sure of it. I am in no way at all, I mean at all, a dancer. I don't even know if you can call what I do dancing. I look more like someone who has lost control of his body, and it's just randomly moving, or like someone running barefoot on hot coals, in pain. It's sad y'all. My first trip with the dance group was to a conference at a church of about 3000 attendees. They had me at the back of the group, and for good reason. I did not know the dance well. At the crescendo of the dance, with a high intensity, we were supposed to punch to the right, then to the left, and then jump with great force. It helped convey the message of the song. I had my head down and was passionately dancing with all my heart. I was dancing like my dance was going to feed all the homeless people in the world. I looked up and realized I totally missed the timing and got caught in the rhythm going the wrong direction. So while everyone was going left, I was going right. I was the only one going a different direction. It was pretty obvious that was not what I was supposed to be doing. After the dance, I felt so embarrassed. It was our first big event, and I blew it.

I thought, "They will never bring me on another trip again." For the the next few moments, I felt so defeated. After service, we were in the green room eating and hanging out. Everyone else was laughing and having a good time. I was not. I felt so overwhelmed by feelings and thoughts of defeat. It took me a moment, and then I looked around and thought, "everyone here is having a good time. I am the only one who is not." I realized I don't have to stay here. In that moment, I chose to not stay in defeat. I shook it off and thanked God for the opportunity. After that, I felt so much better and was able to enjoy the rest of the night. Later on, that service was aired on Trinity Broadcast Network (TBN), and I was able to laugh it off at that point. I had to make the choice to not let defeat become a part of me and get stuck there. I was able to push past the defeat, let joy come forth, and get out of satan's kingdom, the place of defeat.

## DEFEAT WILL HINDER DESTINY

In Numbers 13-14 (NLT), Moses sends spies into Canaan to scout out the land that God wanted them to have. The spies come back with giant grapes and talk about how wonderful this land is that flows with milk and honey. They got the people excited by showing them this great stuff that was there. But all the spies, except Joshua and Caleb, spoke about how they could not take the land because it was too difficult. They spoke with doubt and defeat. That talk of defeat spread like wildfire through the people. The poison of Satan got in the camp. Because of that, God refused to let them in to the promised land and wanted to kill them immediately. Moses interceded on their behalf. God did not kill them in that moment. He did kill all the other spies that let defeat come in to their hearts and spread it to the people. Their defeat caused the Israelites not to enter the promised land in that generation.

Having the poison of defeat become part of us will stop us from entering into the promises that God has for us. Once defeat entered into the camp, there was no way God could let them move forward with that kind of heart. God waited an entire generation out until they died. Then he brought the Israelites in to the land he had for them.

## EFFECTS OF DEFEAT ON A PERSON

Defeat robs from life. It is carrying the heavy burden of failure in your heart. It is feeling the pain of loss and grief before anything is even attempted. At this point, the enemy is positioned to win. Many athletes say sporting events are won or lost before the event beings. It is as much mental as it is physical.

Once defeat wraps itself around you, it begins to squeeze the life of God right out of you. Like a python, it grabs on to its prey and applies sufficient pressure. It prevents the prey from inhaling. With every shallow breath, pressure increases until the breath is gone. It brings you to hopelessness, unmotivated to even try to fight.

To be in defeat is to be in slavery. We will cover slavery thoroughly in another chapter. When an army defeats another army, the losing troops become the winning troops' slaves. We are in the army of the Lord, and he is victorious. So we are victorious by default. When we are not in our rightful position with him, we may not be in the best vantage point. We can't see and demonstrate his victory. God is raising up the army. It's time to get on the side of victory.

---

[2] "Defeat." Dictionary.com. Accessed January 10, 2016. http://www.dictionary.com/browse/defeat?s=t.

[3] *Wikipedia*, s.v. "defeatism," accessed June 2014, https://en.wikipedia.org/wiki/Defeatism.

# three

## SELF-DECEIVED

The devil is self-deceived. That's why he keeps persisting in fighting against God. He keeps thinking that he will win and overthrow God. It's like a cartoon that was popular in the 1990s, *Pinky and the Brain*. They were lab mice, and in every episode they would come up with an elaborate plan to take over the world. Then in each episode, they would fail. Pinky would say to Brain, "What are we going to do tomorrow?" Brain would answer, "The same thing we do every day Pinky, try to take over the world."[4]

> You said in your heart, "I will ascend to the heavens;
> I will raise my throne above the stars of God; I will sit
> enthroned on the mount of assembly, on the utmost
> heights of Mount Zaphon. I will ascend above the tops
> of the clouds; I will make myself like the Most High."
> But you are brought down to the realm of the dead, to
> the depths of the pit. Isaiah 14:13-15 NIV

The enemy has not changed. He is still trying to do what he said in Isaiah 14 (NASB). Every day he is trying to overthrow God. He is persistent because he is delusional. He keeps thinking that he is going to win, so he keeps trying. He will never give up. A part of his plan of overthrowing God is to overthrow us from our place. As believers, we are carriers of God's presence. We are created in the image of God. Satan hates the image of God, so he hates us. He wants to destroy us, and he thinks he can.

The enemy only gains victory over us when we choose to believe him. He is always lying. The lie has no power over us unless we let our guard down. We let our guard down by letting his lies become common in our minds and hearts rather than the truth of God's word. These lies bring defeat and darkness. 1 Peter 5:8 (NASB) tells us, "Your adversary the devil prowls around like a roaring lion, seeking someone to devour." He is looking for an opening to give someone else his defeat.

> The great dragon was hurled down--that ancient serpent called the devil, or Satan, who leads the whole world astray. He was hurled to the earth, and his angels with him. (Revelation 12:9 NIV)

> Your heart became proud on account of your beauty, and you corrupted your wisdom because of your splendor. So I threw you to the earth; I made a spectacle of you before kings. (Ezekiel 28:17 NIV)

You can't give what you don't have. Satan is deceived. The deception is what he has to give. He has deceived himself into thinking he is going to win, but he only has defeat. He wants to deceive us to buy into his defeat.

> Then the devil, who had deceived them, was thrown into the fiery lake of burning sulfur, joining the beast and the false prophet. There they will be tormented day and night forever and ever." (Revelation 20:10 NLT)

God has given us the power over this deceived one that is cast down. Our assignment is to demonstrate and execute the victory of God. As believers, we are ambassadors of the kingdom of God. We have the victory of God over the enemy. We bring the kingdom of God into the earth. We are doorways and portals for God to be active in the earth. We have the ability to bring the things of Heaven into the earth through his impact in our lives. We have been impacted by God. We can now impact others with his Kingdom.

---

[4] "Pinky and the Brain." In Animaniacs. Kids' WB. 1995-1998.

# four

## RELIGIOUS SPIRIT

The Religious Spirit's nature is to use religious activity in the place of intimacy and relationship with Holy Spirit in our life. Its primary goal is to have the church holding to a form of godliness, although they have denied its power. (2 Timothy 3:5 NIV)

The religious spirit is a body without breath in it. It is a human form, yet there is no life; it's a corpse. A true relationship with God is a body filled with breath. It's alive. Religion will lead you to read ten chapters of the Bible. When you are done reading it, you know a lot of information. Yet it has no life in it, and it will produce no fruit in you. In comparison, the Holy Spirit may have you read one verse. That one verse will be life to you in that moment. It applies to right where you are and touches your heart. It will illuminate things in your heart and connect to many areas of your life.

The religious spirit is a hard task master, always demanding and wanting more. I heard a minister say that one night he was reading his Bible before bed, and after he finished one chapter, he closed his Bible. Then he felt something drive him: "Read more. Don't go to bed yet." So he picked up his Bible and kept reading, then he got tired and put the Bible down and was about to go to bed. Then he had this feeling of dread that drove him to read more. After another hour of reading the Bible past his exhaustion, he realized it was not God. It was the religious spirit driving him. It was not restful or joyful; it was torment. The heart of God is to relate and connect with us, not to hurt or abuse us. Reading his Bible hours into the night may look like a good thing at first. When you look closer, you realize it was not producing life, just a form. It was tiring and draining life from him.

The religious spirit is the greatest performer. It knows its lines perfectly. It knows what to do on cue and how to look. It teaches you how to change behavior without changing the heart. Someone functioning under the religious spirit can do all the correct actions on the outside, yet the source is not a changed heart but just the appearance of good. From the outside, you can't identify a religious spirit. It can look the same as the true heart of God. It is great at mimicking the activities of someone in a relationship with God.

## THE RELIGIOUS SPIRIT'S JOB

The religious spirit is a wall that protects the heart from being affected and touched by love. 1 John 4:8 (NIV) says "Whoever does not love does not know God, because God is love." So a religious spirit stops the heart from knowing God, who is love. It allows the heart to know about God, but not encounter and know him. It stops the heart from receiving and giving love. It stops someone from walking in the true power of God's divine love. That love is what transforms the human heart. That love transformed a man from killing Christians into one of the greatest apostles in the New Testament. It is through God's supernatural love that we are touched and changed from the heart. Romans 2:4 (NIV) says that it is the kindness of God that draws our hearts to repentance, which is transformation.

The religious spirit does not add substance or nutritional value to our spiritual life. It's like eating cotton candy. Puffed up, it may taste sweet, but it provides no substance to sustain a spiritual life. It only looks large, but at the first touch of moisture, it disappears. This is the substance of the religious spirit. It feeds and inflates the pride of men, giving it a great appearance. James 4:6 (NKJV) says God resists the proud but gives grace to the humble. If we become proud, God now begins to pull against us. This then puts God in a place of fighting against us, not fighting with us. Then we get more tired and burned out, because who can fight against God and win?

## FEAR AND PRIDE

The religious spirit operates off the foundation of fear and pride. If someone struggles with the fear of failure, the religious spirit will take advantage of it. I know this well because I have had to deal with this in my own life. The fear of failure will partner with the performing nature of the religious spirit. It drives you to strive to never make a mistake. The religious spirit can often identify problems with accuracy, yet it has no solutions to these problems. It operates under the facade of control and manipulation to help you do better. The religious spirit focuses on destroying a relationship with the Lord. It never has the heart to see someone restored. It focuses on judgment and rejection of someone who does not appear to measure up.

One of Jesus' biggest enemies was the religious spirit of his day. The spiritual community was used to doing religious activity without God being present. They had the business of church life down to a formula. They had traditions that they elevated to god status. Once God did show up, he contradicted their system and traditions. God did not fit within their formula. Jesus brought true freedom and life. The religious spirit cannot coexist with the true spirit of God. What did the religious spirit do to Jesus when it met him face to face? It killed him. The religious spirit aggressively pursues the true spirit of God to kill it.

We all have the capacity to fall into operating under a religious spirit. We can start out passionately serving God and then find ourselves in a religious routine. We have to remember that we are serving Jesus and not just a ritual, routine or formula. Don't love what you do more than the One who called you to do it.

## ONE THING THE RELIGIOUS SPIRIT CAN'T REPRODUCE

Pastor Bill Johnson makes a great statement in his book *When Heaven Invades Earth*. He said, "Religion is unable to mimic the life of resurrection with its victory over sin and Hell."[5] I see this to mean it can mimic the acts of Christianity, but it could never mimic the life of one who is full of joy. This joy comes from being transformed. The transformation is from the inside out by an encounter with Jesus. I don't know about you, but

I have never seen a religious person full of joy. They always look bitter and mean. They are usually bold to tell you what you should and should not do, but that is just my observation.

## TEN CHARACTERISTICS OF THE RELIGIOUS SPIRIT

1. Powerlessness. 2 Timothy 3:5 (NKJV) "Having a form of godliness, but denying its power" … Outward expression of godliness, but no inner working
2. Focusing on the Negative. Focus on tearing down what we primarily see as wrong, and always see what is wrong with people, churches, etc.
3. Always trying to fix others
4. Thinking you are closer to God than someone else. God looks at the heart and we can't see the heart
5. Performance. Doing things to be noticed by men
6. Glory in the past things of God and wanting to return to the old things of God
7. Mechanical prayer life. Can't wait till it's done, doing it out of duty, not love
8. Inflexible, can't change anything
9. Perfectionism, can't tolerate mistakes, legalism, regulates and controls everything
10. Excessive guilt which motivates a person to work to be accepted by God[6]

## GREAT COMMERCIAL, BUT A TERRIBLE PRODUCT

The danger with the religious spirit is that it gives us a false sense of doing the right thing. It pacifies our guilt and strokes our ego. I heard someone ministering make a statement about Proverbs 14:12 (NIV), which says "There is a way that appears to be right, but in the end, it leads to death." We often credit the way that seems right to be sin. Yet we all know sin is not right. So could it be talking about religion being the way that may seem right to us? In the end, it produces nothing. It's a dead body, just the form with no life.

The religious spirit has won salesman of the year for centuries. It sells you a product that sounds holy and spiritual. Once you sign on the dotted line, all you get is bondage and a life of fear of not meeting all the requirements. Some trade their slavery to a worldly life for slavery to a religious one. They do this when they convert to Christianity if they have not given up the slavery mentality.

The danger is that one will settle for comfortable religious activity. This choice can cause them to have no impact here in the earth. They have rendered themselves irrelevant by serving the religious spirit.

## MY OWN MANIFESTATION

Here is an example of my personal experience with the religious spirit manifesting in my heart. I was in Bible college and I was in a worship service. I had my hands lifted. A prophetic song came forth. The worship leader was singing a song about God being our heavenly Father. The Lord spoke to me saying, "I want to be your heavenly Father." I said, "That's great Lord, I know that." He said it a few times, and I kept dismissing it. It finally hit me. I realized that I grew up in church hearing that God is our heavenly Father. I thought I understood what it meant. I understood that concept in my head, but it never entered into my heart. I was telling the Lord "I don't need that. I know what it means."

I did not know what it meant in my heart. Puffed up pride in my head was resisting God. He came to encounter my heart with this part of his heart for me. I was rejecting what God was trying to bring to me. In that moment, I broke and began to weep and receive God as my heavenly Father. The moment when we think we know something, we become closed. We cannot receive in the area that we think we know everything. I learned through that experience that I have to be like a little child. I have to always be willing to learn even if it's something I think I understand already. I was able to say, "Lord I have heard this about you, but I need to experience it. I desire that it can be true in my own heart." I left the place of theory for the place of encountering him.

# BREAKING THE RELIGIOUS SPIRIT

To get free from religion you must believe that you can't fix yourself. You are not strong enough to fix yourself. You must plead guilty to your weakness and not try to protect or justify yourself. The fact that you would try to justify yourself and explain your actions means that you think there is an excuse. There is no excuse that God will accept. The only redemption you have is to fall on Jesus from your weakness and let him cover you and set you right, by his power.

Ephesians 2:8 (NKJV) says "For by grace you have been saved through faith, and that not of yourselves; it is the gift of God, ..." Also, Romans 3:20 tells us "Therefore by the deeds of the law no flesh will be justified in His sight, for by the law is the knowledge of sin." We can't save ourselves by our works; it is only by his grace. Yielding to the Lord is the only answer. Yielding causes us to live our lives out of our love for him. We follow God's law out of our love, not out of following a list of dos and don'ts to make ourselves right. We must live from the heart and not the head.

---

[5] Johnson, Bill. When Heaven Invades Earth: A Practical Guide to a Life of Miracles. Shippensburg, PA: Treasure House, 2003.
[6] "4 MAJOR CHARACTERISTICS OF A RELIGIOUS SPIRIT." 4 MAJOR CHARACTERISTICS OF A RELIGIOUS SPIRIT. June 29, 1997. Accessed November 04, 2014. http://www.angelfire.com/sd/sermons/RELIGION3.htm.

# five

## SLAVERY MENTALITY

slave noun \'slāv\
1 a person held in servitude as the chattel of another
2 one that is completely subservient to a dominating influence
3 a device (as the printer of a computer) that is directly responsive to another
4 drudge, toiler
someone who is legally owned by another person and is forced to work for that person without pay
5 a person who is strongly influenced and controlled by something.[7]

Above we see the definition of the word slave. It is to be under the dominating or controlling influence of someone or something else. It's a person who does not make choices for his or her own life, but feels someone or something else makes those choices. Satan desires to make us slaves. He wants to rule our lives. If we give in and become slaves, then a slavery mentality will fill our lives.

Harriet Tubman led many slaves to freedom through the Underground Railroad. She said this about the slavery mentality: "I freed a thousand slaves. I would've freed a thousand more, if they only knew they were slaves." The attitude of slavery is that slaves think the situation is unchangeable. Therefore they never try to fight against it. Slaves start to operate within the system instead of above it. We have to

19

become aware of the works of slavery. You cannot unlock some slaves' chains if they claim they don't have any.

I heard a powerful message from my spiritual covering Apostle Jane Hamon about slavery mentality. She gave the definition of slave mentality as this: People conditioned to quietly, and without objection, accept harmful circumstances for themselves as the natural order of things. They're also conditioned to accept their master's view and beliefs about themselves. They strive to get others within their group to accept the master's view. It becomes embedded generation after generation.

For slaves, this translates into the thinking, "my parents were slaves, and my grandparents were slaves, so I don't hope for anything better." For believers, this could sound like "My mother had depression, and my grandmother had depression. I guess I will just have to deal with this every day of my life." You can replace the word "depression" for whatever is personal to you, like poverty, sickness, addiction, anger, fear, pride, etc. It's just a different mouse trap that keeps you bound.

## SLAVES LIVE WITH INFERIORITY

Slaves live with a sense of inferiority. When Israel had to give a report about the enemy, they said "we are like grasshoppers in their sight." They saw themselves as poor, weak, dependent, not smart enough, not educated enough. Slaves live with hopelessness and expect defeat. They often see this as their way of life and think it's how the entire world is. They have no concept of freedom nor hope for it.

Someone who has embraced the slavery mentality may say phrases like these:

... That's just life.
... This is the way it will always be.
... Some people have it and others don't.
... It's not fair; some people have so much.
... It's not meant to be for me.
... Don't rock the boat; we are lucky we have it the way we do.
... Don't bother the devil, and he won't bother you.
... Try not to be seen; we don't want the attention of the enemy.

… It will never change.

## SYSTEM OF SLAVERY

> Jones relates conversations he had with his grandfather, who was born 1861, … Most slaves didn't have any concept of freedom because being slaves was all they knew. Rather than being free, the fantasies they harbored was about living in the big house, and being the master. Jones' grandfather had said to him slaves didn't want to be free. They wanted to be the master.[8]

The slavery system is meant to destroy you. It is designed to tear you down and not allow you to rise above it. When it has reached it's desired result, you no longer want freedom. You want to climb the ranks of the system to be the slave master. You then become a part of the system and tear others down. After your hope and desire to be free is killed, you become a slave master. You then view others as less than as an excuse to enslave them. Hilter could only convince people to hate and kill Jews when he dehumanized the Jews. The same happened with African Americans in the times of slavery. Slaves are dehumanized in the eyes of the slave owners. Once you dehumanize someone, you can treat that person in any way because he or she is less than you. Yet we were all made in the image of God and called to live as such.

People who have been defeated for too long will try to become the slave master of others and try to oppress them. They want to kill the desire for freedom they now see in someone else. This is because another's desire and will for freedom is confronting the now dead areas of desiring freedom in themselves. If they were to acknowledge their desire for freedom, they would then have to face their own guilt of giving up and adopting the slavery system. It is often easier to try to get someone stuck in your bondage than to get help out of your own bondage.

It requires more energy to start a motion that you are not doing. It is easier to go into auto-pilot and keep doing what you are already doing. People can be locked up in slavery and still be free on the inside if they have not let the mentality take over their minds. Yet people who are free in their external position can mentally be slaves. They might as well have the chains on their hands and feet. Being a slave in chains can be overcome once a person breaks and is set free from an external situation. Once the poison becomes internal, no matter what the person does, he or she is still in prison, carrying the bondage internally.

Slaves cannot fight what enslaves them because they are inexperienced in war. Chances are that a person became enslaved because he or she did not have the ability internally to defeat what enslaved him or her.

## GETTING STUCK

Slavery tries to get people to the point of giving up. If their will to fight breaks, they accept the system of slavery. Then they may become resistant to change. People with slavery mentality may develop pride. It looks like they failed, so they may not want anyone else to try. If someone else succeeds, it looks bad on the one who gave up. The enthusiasm and passion of the one who tries to escape only confronts the apathy of the people with slavery mentality. So they grow to hate what comes into their world, even though it could bring the life that they so desperately need. They become the persecutors of the very thing that will bring freedom. Hence freedom can never be achieved.

A big lie we accept is the "one day" lie. It goes like this: One day things will be different. One day I will be free, wealthy, healthy, and living the dream. You may say, "That's not a lie. One day things *will* get better." The problem with that is things will never be different until we change it. Things will never be different tomorrow if we are not choosing differently today. We must rise up and make deliberate choices that will make our future look different than our present.

## DESIRING BONDAGE

But you were unwilling to go up; you rebelled against the command of the Lord your God. You grumbled in your tents and said, "The Lord hates us; so he brought us out of Egypt to deliver us into the hands of the Amorites to destroy us. Where can we go? Our brothers have made our hearts melt in fear. They say, 'The people are stronger and taller than we are; the cities are large, with walls up to the sky. We even saw the Anakites there.'" (Deuteronomy 1:26-28 NIV)

The Israelites were now free from Egypt, but when they encountered a conflict, they wanted to go back to slavery. They adopted slavery as their way of life. They had been slaves for so long that they did not know freedom was an option. The only success they saw was to succeed in the structure already in place. Even if they were free, they would have no idea where to even start, because all they knew was bondage.

It is one thing to lose a game or one event. It's another thing to be defeated in your spirit and soul. If you are defeated there, you will accept defeat as your reality. If your mind is filled with defeat, then you will never even get up and try to fight. So many are defeated by believing they have already lost. Every time you get up and get back in the battle, you win.

## YOU DON'T HAVE TO BE A SLAVE

Joseph was in the system of slavery, but he never became a slave. He functioned in the structure of slavery as a free man. Physically, he was in slavery, but in his heart, he did not give into defeat and became a slave. Joseph worked as hard in prison as he would have if it was his own business. Joseph was so faithful that the prison guards put him in charge of taking care of the needs of the prison: "The warden paid no attention to anything under Joseph's care because the LORD was with Joseph and gave him success in whatever he did" (Genesis 39:23 NIV). Despite his circumstances, he was able to prosper. Your circumstance can't make you a slave, but giving up in your heart can. Joseph held on to the word of the Lord in his heart.

When our vision is based on our circumstances and what we have in our hands, our faith will not rise at all. Our vision has to be based on what is in God's hand. Break free from your limitations. If you are living with bondage, change it! It's time for a revolt from slavery.

The way we break out is by believing God. Once you believe what

God has said about you and about your circumstance, you lose all doubt. No matter what you see in front of you, what God says has to be inside of you without a doubt. What you are fighting, more than anything else, is the fight to believe God. Our struggle is believing the natural versus believing the supernatural.

Slaves always feel limited: "I am limited in my success because of … " Slaves believe they cannot change the future. They see the future as something that happens to them. I declare you are breaking free of this and are one that will shape the future by the word of the Lord. By the power of God's Spirit in you, you can change your situation!

---

[7] Merriam-Webster. Accessed January 10, 2015. https://www.merriam-webster.com/dictionary/slave.

[8] Teeth, Hell's. "Slave Mentality." Hell's Teeth:. 1970. Accessed June 04, 2016. http://mewlop.blogspot.com/2009/06/slave-mentality.html.

# six

## VICTIM MENTALITY

The victim mentality is an acquired (learned) personality trait. It is where a person tends to regard him or herself as a victim of the negative actions of others. They behave like it was the case—even in the absence of clear evidence. It depends on habitual thought processes and attribution.[9]

What stands out to me the most about a victim mentality is that it is a learned behavior. The enemy desires to teach us to be victims. People with this mentality will view any negative event as permanent. They will also see it aimed at them personally. They see the world as against them. They are number one on everyone's hit list. People with this mindset have many obstacles to overcome. Most of the obstacles are self-imposed. I know we are talking about a friend of yours, not you of course.

## FIVE THINGS THAT EFFECT A PERSON WITH A VICTIM MENTALITY

1. See it hard to trust God or godly authority
2. Live in constant fear and jealousy
3. Cannot accept personal responsibility
4. Unable to appreciate what they already have
5. Feel they do not have a choice of what happens to them.[10]

When we see ourselves as the underdog, we have the victim mentality. We feel like we have more to overcome than everyone else to do the same task. If we have this mentality, we subconsciously make choices that lead us deeper into being a victim.

## THE VICTIM MENTALITY IS SELF-FULFILLING

When we learn the skill of being a victim, it shapes how we act. We start acting like a victim, and victim situations will play out over and over in our lives. If we do not recognize that this is an assignment from the enemy, we adopt being a victim as our belief system. Proverbs 23:7 (NKJV) says "For as he thinks in his heart, so is he." That belief in your heart, I mean your friend's heart, will cause that person to live out a victim reality.

One of the greatest miracles is that God took a bunch of slaves and turned them into a bunch of warriors. He taught them to defeat armies and nations. God had to break their victim mindset to get them to this point. Some still wanted to be a victim. They were complaining that they ever left Egypt, despite all that they had seen and experienced. You can experience great miracles and still be a victim in your heart. Your outside circumstance is not what creates the victim mentality. What is in the heart does. At the heart level, you must reject being a victim and choose freedom.

## VICTIMS CAN'T SEE MIRACLES

The Israelites were slaves for hundreds of years and came into a victim mentality. At one point in their transition from being victims to being victors, they complained about their process to freedom. We see this played out in Exodus 14:11 (NIV). The Israelites were facing the Red Sea with the Egyptian armies behind them. They said to Moses, "You brought us to the desert to die? Aren't there graves in Egypt? You could have left us there." Despite all the miracles they had already experienced, they still saw themselves as victims. They saw the negative situation that they were facing as permanent.

The Israelites were being pursued by one of the greatest armies on the planet. They are not soldiers, but slaves. They knew they did not have the skill set needed to defend themselves. Then, of course, they walked right up to the Red Sea. Now they knew for sure it was over. This would be where it ends. Everything up to now was pointless. There was no need for them to be brought through all the ten plagues. It got their hopes up, only for it to all end right here. They immediately saw themselves as victims again.

Then God leads Moses to stretch forth his rod over the water. Moses does as God asks, and God parts the water. They cross over on dry ground. Then the Egyptian army comes after them. I am sure if this was today, somebody would have been taking pictures and posting on social media. Once the Israelites crossed over, God sent the water back. It killed all the Egyptians that were chasing after them. This was a two-fold miracle. God set the Israelites free and killed their enemies all in one miracle. Where the Israelites were looking at the situation as victims, God had a plan to bring them into victory. They could not imagine the Red Sea working for them. They could only see it working against them. God is working in your life, setting you up for victory. If you have a victim mentality, you can only view it as something working against you.

## THE WAY OF ESCAPE

Romans 8:28 (AMP) "We are assured and know that [God being a partner in their labor] all things work together and are [fitting into a plan] for good to and for those who love God and are called according to [His] design and purpose." God was working all things for Israel's good. They perceived through their victim mindset that this was another bad thing happening to them. They did not realize God was partnering with them. It was a great setup for victory on their behalf.

So many of us have given our lives over to being led by whatever happens to us. We live day to day depending on things to just work out for us. Victims look to be carried through life by someone else, such as government, God, parents, a spouse, or whatever it may be. God did not call us to be victims of life and to have passivity. God has called us to be active participators in the life he has given us. We are called to partner with Him. We must choose to actively take part. In Deuteronomy 30:19

27

(NIV) God says he gives us a choice to choose blessing or cursing. We choose. We are not victims of our circumstances.

> "Self-pity is easily the most destructive of the nonpharmaceutical narcotics; it is addictive, gives momentary pleasure and separates the victim from reality." John W. Gardner[11]

> "If it's never our fault, we can't take responsibility for it. If we can't take responsibility for it, we'll always be its victim." Richard Bach[12]

# THREE KEYS TO BREAK THE VICTIM MENTALITY

## 1.) TAKE RESPONSIBILITY FOR YOUR LIFE.

If you don't take responsibility for your own life, you might be led somewhere you don't want to go. A reason you might avoid taking responsibility is the feeling that you could fail, and you would have no one else to blame but yourself. That may be true, but you will definitely fail if you don't try.

You have to take back control of your life and not be a victim of what's going to happen in it. You declare and partner with what God says about your life. God has given us our lives to steward and manage with the tools he has given us of prayer, worship and the Word.

## 2.) GIVE THANKS

Give thanks for what you have, not being concerned with what you don't have. Gratitude will help you take your view off of yourself and place it on God. It will shift your mindset and cause you to have a more positive outlook.

## 3.) FORGIVE

Let go of anyone or anything that has hurt you. Yes, I understand the pain and the hurt is real. However, if you don't forgive, you will always have the pain and hurt and will never heal. Not forgiving is like locking yourself in a room with your greatest fear and deciding to live there. Forgive and set yourself free to not be a victim.

---

[9] "Victim Mentality." Wikipedia. Accessed June 04, 2016. https://en.m.wikipedia.org/wiki/Victim_mentality.

[10] Hamon, Thomas S. "Spiritual Authority." Lecture, Understanding Spiritual Authority, Vision Church Christian International, Santa Rosa Beach. December 2014. Accessed December/January 2015. http://www.ministrytrainingcollege.com/courses/spiritual-authority/.

[11] "Translation." John W. Gardner: Self-pity Is Easily the Most Destructive of the Non-pharmaceutical Narcotics; It Is Addictive, Gives Momentary Pleasure and Separates the Victim from Reality. Accessed August 04, 2015. http://www.quotes.net/quote/51653.

[12] "Richard Bach Quotes." BrainyQuote. Accessed August 04, 2015. http://www.brainyquote.com/quotes/quotes/r/richardbac389113.html.

# seven

## FATALISM

Fatalism is the belief that whatever will be will be; "Que sera sera." It means that fate decides for us.

[Fatalism] is a philosophical doctrine holding that all events are predetermined in advance, they are inevitable, for all time and man has no power to change them, Included in this is that man has no power to influence the future, or indeed, his own actions.[13]

Fatalism is one of those things that is a punch straight to the chest, which has the ability to knock the wind out of you. Fatalism says it is pointless to keep pushing for something to change because the outcome is already determined. What's happening is happening. It's like when we say, "It is what it is."

An experiment was done by Charisse Nixon, PH. D Developmental Psychologist at Penn Sate Erie. She handed out sheets of paper, with a list of three words on it, to her classroom. For each word, the students had to rearrange the letters and spell another word using all the letters of that word. They would come up with three new words. She gave the class a few minutes to do the assignment. Then she said "raise your hand once you are done." Half the class raised their hand, and the other half looked around very confused. When time was up to finish the assignment, half the class still had not finished. She explained to the class what they just experienced. The class had two different lists of words on their paper. Half the class had a list on which the first two words could not be rearranged to make another word. The other half had a list where all three words could be rearranged to make another word.

The group that was given the list on which the first two words could not be rearranged did not solve the third word on their page either, even though it was an easy word to rearrange. The students were asked how they felt while trying to figure out the answer, once they realized that they could not solve the answer. They explained that they felt frustrated and angry that they were not able to come up with an answer. Then when the teacher said to raise their hands if they were finished, it made them feel not as smart as the other students in the room when they saw half the room had hands in the air. Many said they gave up at that point, feeling like they were not able to figure it out. They did not even try the third word because they felt defeated by the first two words. Many looked at themselves as flawed: "I am not as smart as others, so there is no reason to keeping trying." The first two things that the students faced were impossible situations. This situation paralyzed them from moving forward by making them not willing to even try the third word.[14]

The students whose first two words were unsolvable accepted fatalism. They might not adopt it as their life philosophy, but in that moment, they accepted it for that situation. They did not attempt the third word because they now believed they can do nothing to solve this problem. They believed this is just the way it is.

Once you have consistently encountered disappointment, you can start to see disappointment as the way it should be. You can learn fatalism from your personal situations. You may have been like the students in that classroom. You encountered difficult situations at a young age, and when you looked around, things seemed easy for everyone else. You may have come to the conclusion that things just don't work for you. That failure at a young age may have paralyzed you from ever being willing to try again. The pain of past failures can lead us into a mindset of fatalism.

## LEARNED HELPLESSNESS

There is a concept called learned helplessness:

> Learned helplessness is a technical term that refers to
> the condition of a human or animal that has learned

to behave helplessly, failing to respond even though there are opportunities for it to help itself by avoiding unpleasant circumstances or by gaining positive rewards. may result from a perceived absence of control over the outcome of a situation.[15]

In other words, learned helplessness is not trying to get out of a negative situation because the past has taught you that you are helpless. All you need is one disappointment to cause you to shut down and refuse to get up and try again. The enemy does not have to keep oppressing you after you choose fatalism. All he had to do was set up one or two situations in your life that seemed too difficult, so that by the third situation, you had already given up.

I have heard this story a few times, but I think it paints an accurate picture of how defeat breaks your will to change things. A circus took a baby elephant and tied one end of a rope around its leg and the other end around a metal stake in the ground. The baby elephant pulled every day with all its might, but the stake would not budge. Freedom was not an option. The baby elephant gave up on trying to pull free from the stake. It now knew it could not break free from this stake in the ground. The elephant continued to grow and get stronger, but the stake never changed. By the time the elephant was fully grown, it would take minimal effort to pull the stake out of the ground; however, the elephant was conditioned not to try, even though it now had the power to pull free.

In learned helplessness, an individual that is regularly exposed to a negative outcome will eventually stop trying to push past the negative thing and will behave as though utterly helpless to change the situation. When the opportunity to escape presents itself, this person has no ability to take action. The only way to cope once in this state is to not expect anything positive to happen at all. Even after the original situation has changed, and whatever has caused one to enter this state of fatalism is gone, the damage is already done to the soul. That one will need inner healing from the trauma that brought learned helplessness in.

# THE TRAP

Everyone experiences difficult times, so the key is to not get stuck there. You cannot choose to camp out there and never move forward from that moment of defeat and pain.

Fatalism has many ways of getting us to buy into it. Others around us can help create an atmosphere that makes it easier to buy into it. If we see others give in to defeat, then we can start to say, "Well if no one else is trying, why should I?" Or out of wanting to fit in and not stand out, we can pull back because it's easier to swim with the current than swim against it. Or we may see someone else fail and not want to fail also, so we decide not to try. We can also listen to the negativity of others and think, "They must know more than I do." Or we may try to do something and have others speak words of doubt to us. If we receive those words, it can fill us with fatalism and cause us to give up.

When we give into fatalism, we become mostly passive. We could also have a lot of anxiety about everything that could possibly go wrong. We may become more untrusting of people and then isolate from people and even from God.

Fatalism also affects our problem-solving ability. Once we hit a crisis, we will view it as final and think no good thing can come out of it. So defeat already begins to settle in and stop us from making the best choices to bring a positive outcome. We feel like we are in the middle of uncontrollable circumstances, and it leaves us paralyzed and unable to make good choices to move forward.

Fatalism is the deep rooted feeling that our actions will produce no results. It sounds like this: "No matter how much or how hard I work, I never have enough money," or "No matter how much I work out, I never lose weight." A person with a strong self-will to strive will keep doing the task in this environment, while being depressed and discouraged. This person doesn't know what else to do except keep going, even while believing things will never change. A person without the strong drive to strive will just give up and let anything happen. This person may loose desire to get out of bed in the morning or may not be motivated to do anything. Neither response is a good one.

Fatalism could also come from being driven toward an internal goal that is not realistic. This person is living to get to some goal that is a fantasy. It could be someone who desires to get married, but he or she has a checklist that the potential spouse has to meet, a checklist so specific that the only way to get this spouse is to build him or her in a lab. It is an internal goal with no external answer to meet that goal. So he or she lives wishing to meet this fantasy person, but all his or her efforts produce no results because that person does not exist. Working to get to a fantasy goal will perpetuate the feeling that things will never change.

Fatalism also comes from feeling out of control. When you perceive events as uncontrollable and unpredictable, you are less likely to have hope that you can change things. You will also stop looking for opportunities to change your situation. It will cause you to be demotivated.

Once you have received fatalism, it will then cause you to become pessimistic. Pessimism is a state of mind in which one anticipates negative outcomes. This view will make you a critical person. You then move from seeing things that way for yourself to becoming someone that releases pessimism to others and brings them into that place also.

There are probably some areas in your life that you think are impossible, yet they may have the ability to change. Sometimes when a webpage is not working, you just have to hit the refresh button and try again. Once you do that, the page loads with no problem. Your situations are the same way. Sometimes we have to refresh and try again.

## FATALISM CAUSED BY SURROUNDINGS

We can learn fatalism from our surroundings. You can see this in the people from different environments. Someone who was born and raised in an urban city like New York and someone from a small rural town in Alabama have different outlooks. They both have only experienced maybe a fifty-mile radius from where they live. But they have formed a concrete opinion of what the world is like and what is possible. They have let their environment train them. It conditioned them to think in the way their environment works, and they cannot see beyond that. They have no concept that someone may live differently than they do. Young people that are born and raised in an urban culture may believe rap songs and believe that lifestyle is the only way to live because that is all they have been exposed to. I recently heard a famous rapper in an interview say that he does not drink or smoke, or even believe in the lifestyle he raps about. He sees it as an entertainment and business. He says that he is playing a character. I find this interesting that he is helping to indoctrinate an entire generation about a lifestyle that he does not believe in at all. Then inner-city youth learn through this culture and music that this is what life is all about. If they don't get exposed to something else, they will live their lives like this and never know there is more than what they have experienced.

I grew up in the Bronx, New York, in a Jamaican part of town. I was surrounded by Jamaicans everywhere. When I would walk down the street, I saw Jamaican flags, heard Jamaican music, and smelled Jamaican restaurants. No one in our neighborhood went out jogging. No one went to fine restaurants or watched Shakespeare plays. Just about ten miles away was Central Park. Central Park is the center of New York city. People jogged through the park. They watched Shakespeare in the park. People in the park did not wear baggy pants. Just ten miles aways were people who lived completely different lives. We lived in a different world and formed different world views. They did not know our world, and we did not know theirs. When we adopt a fatalistic mindset, we never see a world with hope, where things can change and get better.

What we have experienced is not everything. We must not become trapped by our disappointments. We must not build our world around our failures. It can feel easier to give in to fatalism than to fight it. You are right; it is easier to give in because there is no resistance when you give in to it. The resistance comes when you are fighting to get out of it. It is like being a pioneer who is just entering a jungle. Every step is a new territory, and you have to cut your way through it. Fatalism has a path already created, and you can fall in it and be lulled to sleep. God has called us to be pioneers and trailblazers.

We are made in the image of God, and God's nature is to create. Our nature is to create. We are not meant to just let life happen to us. We are created to create; we were made to push against resistance.

# KEYS FOR BREAKING OUT OF FATALISM

Proverbs 18:21 (NASB) says that death and life are in the power of the tongue. Our tongue has creative power and is a force for either good or evil. We can agree with what our environment or situation is speaking to us, or we can agree with God.

Psalms 42:11 (NKJV) says, "Why are you cast down, O my soul? And why are you disquieted within me? Hope in God; For I shall yet praise Him, The help of my countenance and my God." Here David talks to himself. He is speaking to his soul to rise up and trust in God, not in the situation that he sees around him. Sometimes you might have to talk to yourself. We must choose to believe God rather than our situation.

We fall into fatalism when we put our belief in this natural world. When we trust our natural perception, we then believe that what we are experiencing in the natural realm is what is true and real. Once we believe it's what is true and real, it then governs our actions. At the point it begins to govern our actions, it becomes our god. We know it becomes our god because we then live our lives based on its rules rather than God's truth. We must be like David and command our soul to trust in God and not what looks like doom and gloom.

> Then this message came to Isaiah from the Lord: "Go back to Hezekiah and tell him, 'This is what the Lord, the God of your ancestor David, says: I have heard your prayer and seen your tears. I will add fifteen years to your life. (Isaiah 38:4-5 NLT)

Hezekiah cried out to God, and fifteen years were added to his life. Hezekiah did not just accept his fate. He believed there was more than what was before him. He trusted in God, and it changed his situation.

> "For I know the plans I have for you," declares the LORD, "plans to prosper you and not to harm you, plans to give you hope and a future. (Jeremiah 29:11 NIV)

We quote this scripture many times. However, what we may miss is that this scripture is given during a hard time for the nation. They were facing absolute destruction. It's not saying everything around will be perfect. It is saying that in the middle of what is destruction, God still has a plan for your good. While we are living our daily lives, if things don't look like what we expect or even want, we must learn to trust God, and know that his plan is for our good. Everything may not make sense or be the best situation, but God is still on our side, and we must press in to him and trust he is working in our life to produce good.

It is not *que sera sera*. Fate does not decide. We are not the products of our environments; we are the products of God's working in our lives to produce his good plan and purpose. We trust in God and believe his best for us. We are partnering with God for his best to be released into the earth.

Jesus gathered his disciples together and sent them out two by two in Mark 6:13. They drove out many demons and anointed many sick people with oil and healed them. Jesus sent them to bring impact to the world around them. They were not called to be passive and just let "life" happen, but to go and impact the lives they encountered.

God used Jonah to help bring a nation to repentance. When God saw what they did and how they turned from their evil ways, he relented and did not bring on them the destruction he had threatened. Jonah partnered with God to help change a nation (Jonah 3:10 NLT).

Abraham was able to work with God to discover what would be the lowest number of righteous people that would have to be in the city for God not to destroy it (Genesis 18: 16-19 NLT).

God wants us to partner with Him. We have a part to play with God. We are called to bring impact to the world.

[13] "The Definition of Fatalism." Dictionary.com. Accessed August 04, 2015. http://www.dictionary.com/browse/fatalism.

[14] Zooeygirl. "Learned Helplessness." YouTube. 2007. Accessed October 04, 2016. https://www.youtube.com/watch?v=gFmFOmprTt0. Shot by Mark Steensland

[15] "How Seligman's Learned Helplessness Theory Applies to Human Depression and Stress." Psychology 104: Social Psychology. Accessed September 04, 2015. http://education-portal.com/academy/lesson/how-seligmans-learned-helplessness-theory-applies-to-human-depression-and-stress.html#lesson.

# eight

## THE SCARCITY MENTALITY

scarcity |'skersitē|
noun (pl. scarcities)
the state of being scarce or in short supply; shortage: a
time of scarcity | the growing scarcity of resources.[16]

In this chapter, we confront another mentality that brings us into defeat: scarcity mentality. As defined above, scarcity means the short supply of resources.

It is human nature to get nervous when you see resources running low, especially if there is no sign of more around. The retail industry knows how to play on that feeling. Advertisements say "seventy percent sale, while supplies last." I am guilty of falling for this. I come home from the store and show my wife what I bought, and she says "Do you need that? Why did you by that.?" I then respond, "well it was a good deal, it's on sale." Then she shakes her head, and I keep making up reasons that it was a good idea. It was not the price that was driving me, but rather the fear of not having it in the future. I was responding to the panic that I am not able to control how much there is and could miss out.

Not having a natural human need met, like food or water, can be scary. It can cause you to respond out of pure emotion and act beyond any reason. It puts you in survival mode. This is being willing to do whatever you can to survive. You feel out of control. We see this during times of natural disasters and civil unrest.

This is one side of the coin of scarcity. The flip side of the coin is that it can paralyze someone from doing anything at all. The feeling of trying to survive because there is not enough may cause someone to bunker down. This person builds a fort and tries to hold on for dear life. They are hoping that they make it. They try to protect everything they have and will not let anyone get close, fearing that person wants what they have. This happens on an individual level or a national level. On a national level, it manifests as a paralyzed economy or a recession. People are afraid to spend money. Companies are afraid to hire or expand the business. Individuals are afraid to start their own business. The economy gets paralyzed, and money stops changing hands. Things get lockup because there seems to not be enough.

## ROOTED IN FEAR

The scarcity mentality is the mindset of not having enough. It is the feeling of impending doom because of a lack of resources. This mentality is rooted in fear. It is a fear of not being valued enough to have your needs taken care of. So it leads someone to have to defend and provide for him or herself. If you have this mentality, it is difficult to watch others receive something you desire. You have the feeling that they got it at a loss to you. It is like there is one life vest on the boat, and if someone else gets it, you won't, and you will sink. "Not enough" is the voice of scarcity.

The scarcity mentally will trap you in self-preservation and survival. It keeps you away from life and living. It gets you trying to out-do others to survive. When someone has a closed hand and is not willing to open it, only what is in that closed hand is what they will posses, which will not be enough to sustain them for a long period of time.

## POVERTY

When we hear the word poverty, we think of not having enough money or resources. That is true if you look at the basic definition of the word, but there is another place you can have poverty. You can have poverty in the soul. I believe poverty in the soul is far worse than poverty in possessions. Poverty is not just having little to no money. It is actually accepting a mindset of limited possibilities. It is being governed by a mindset of lack. You begin to view the world through eyes of what is not possible. Scarcity rules your life.

## SCARCITY ISOLATES

The scarcity mentality will stop us from succeeding. It will stop our God-given potential. It will stop us from working with others and sharing our resources with one another. It will stop us from trusting each other. It will stop us from being willing to unite to meet our individual needs. It will cause us to be divided within the kingdom.

Scarcity causes us to kill the seeds that are in our hands. We kill them by not releasing them. The seed is just a seed when we keep it in our hands. Once we release that seed into the ground, it then has the potential to become a tree. It can produce fruit with a multitude of more seeds. This is the abundance mentality, releasing the seed to produce a multitude of resources. The seed does not just contain a tree, but an entire orchard. It can produce unlimited resources.

I love the model of Christian International to equip the saints to do the work of the ministry. This is an example of releasing the seed into the ground. It seems like you give up the thing you have in your hand. But it actually multiplies beyond you. If you hold on to what you have, that's all you will ever have. There will be no room to grow. If you equip others, they will then create an abundance of resources and outlets. You will grow and they will grow. I heard someone say that in God's kingdom, you only get to keep what you give away.

## GIVE OUT OF SCARCITY

In 1 Kings 17 (NASB) God tells Elijah to go to Zarephath. God has instructed a widow there to feed him. When Elijah gets there, he does not find a woman with a banqueting table, nor with the finest of food, standing there waiting to feed him by hand. He finds a widow woman preparing to die. She had a plan to use the last of her resources to sustain herself and then die. At the beginning of the scripture, God told Elijah to go there: "I have commanded a widow women there to sustain you." How could this be possible, when it looked like she had nothing? It was possible because Elijah was carrying in his mouth the prophetic word. That word would break her and himself out of their scarcity situation. God sent Elijah to interrupt her plan. In that moment, she had a choice to continue to operate with scarcity or not. This encounter with Elijah was an invitation to break out of scarcity mentality and into abundance. If she kept what she had, the plan would have played out just like she had planned it. Instead, she responded to the prophetic word and was set free from scarcity into abundance.

The widow woman had to take inventory of what she had. Then she had to use what she had as seed to sow for what she needed. She had to be willing to open her hand and give what she wanted most desperately to hold on to.

## KEYS TO BREAKING SCARCITY MENTALITY

1. Appreciate what you do have
2. Give away what you feel like you don't have enough to give away

You are a limited resource. If you keep holding on to the little that you have, you will starve to death. The hand that is tightly gripping what it has is also the same hand that will never receive because it has no room to receive. Once that hand opens to give, it is also open to receiving. The way to break a scarcity mentality is to give what you are afraid of losing. Once you are open to giving, you will create an atmosphere of abundance. If you give, you w ill be given to.

Scarcity is rooted in fear. First John 4:18 says that perfect love casts our fear. Abundance is rooted in love. We have to be grounded in the love of God to operate from abundance.

## ABUNDANCE MENTALITY

God wants us to have an abundance mentality. We are to live out of his abundance, not out of our limited realm of humanity. We were never designed to sustain ourselves. God wants us to be ambassadors who live out of the resources of our spiritual nation. We are representing his kingdom nation. The United States sends ambassadors around the world. Those ambassadors do not submit to the resources of that nation. They operate out of the resources of the United States. We are kingdom people. We live out of Heaven's resources.

An abundance mentality tells us that there are always new chances and opportunities. It is the ability to trust God. We move into an abundance mentality by trusting God with our needs. At this place of trust, we get to partake of his unlimited resources. Philippians 4:19 (NASB) tells us that God will supply every need you have according to his riches in glory in Christ Jesus. This assures us God's got it taken care of. From this place, we can rest and trust. We don't have to depend on our own limited potential but can trust in God's unending supply for our needs. In the Greek, the word riches means experience and circumstance. In other words, God will take care of what you need from his experience and from his circumstance, not from yours. His experience is abundance. He knows no lack because he does not have lack. His circumstance is "I am what sustains me and therefore I am what will sustain you. I am the source of sustaining." This is what God is saying.

In our materialistic culture, we are often judged on the things that we posses, things like money, houses, cars and the latest smartphones. Measuring ourselves by these things can lead us to think that God is not supplying our needs since we may not have the latest and the greatest of something that we desire. I recently saw a sitcom in which a man took a long time to make a sandwich for himself just the way he liked it. He placed it on the coffee table, sat down ready to eat, and then realized that he forgot his drink. He got up and went back to the kitchen to get his drink. When he returned to the table, the sandwich was gone. He had about six people living in his house and did not know who took it. So he took the empty plate down to the police station and asked them to dust it for fingerprints. The cop said, "Sir, we can't do that." He said "Why? You're not doing anything. Ya'll just drive around giving out tickets. You should be happy I am giving you something to do." The cop looked back at him and said, "Sir have you ever been beaten to death on the doorstep of your house?" The guy said no. The cop replied, "Then you see that we are busy working." We can miss how God is taking care of us if we look for something different or bigger than what he is doing. Once we set our heart to be in gratitude, we can transition to living out of an abundance mentality.

In an abundance mentality, you are at peace because you know that God supplies all of your needs. It is also easier to see the areas in your life in which God is providing for you. You have joy and peace because you know that you are not on your own. You have the unlimited resources of Heaven to take care of every need that you have. If it has to come from the mouth of a fish, or from a pentecostal handshake, or be left on your doorstep from an unknown source, it doesn't matter; your needs are met. You are a part of a kingdom with unlimited resources.

## GIVING MEETS YOUR NEEDS

My wife and I went to lunch one day at a local pizza place. When we walked in, we saw a table with several police officers eating lunch. In my heart I felt a great sense of appreciation for them. I did not pay much attention to the thought. Then my wife said to me, "We should pay for their lunch." I thought "Yeah, that's a God idea. I feel like that would be a blessing to them." At that moment we did not have a lot of money in our bank account. It was a time between paychecks. My natural thinking would normally be that since it's a few more days until our next paycheck, we should not be giving extra money away. But I knew in my heart that it was God's desire to bless those officers. I let go of the temptation to hold on to scarcity. We asked the server to give us their bill when it was time for them to pay. I later saw her telling the officers that we paid for their lunch. Then the officers came by our table and graciously thanked us and shook our hands. It felt great to give and express God's heart. Later the server came and gave us our bill. She said "The officers get a 50% discount on their meals. I have given you that discount also." So our bill ended up being a few dollars more than Rebecca and I would normally have paid. Then she even gave us a punch card to get a free lunch for next time we came in. We got blessed for being a blessing. Later that same day, someone gave Rebecca and me a $100 gift card to one of our favorite restaurants. I believe all of this was tied to our willingness to have an open heart and hand. Our abundance mentality produced abundance in our life.

---

[16] Accessed November 12, 2015. https://en.oxforddictionaries.com/definition/scarcity.

# nine

## LIES

Two things are constantly battling for our attention whether or not we are aware. That battle is lies versus truth. The fight is to see what we will choose to believe.

## THE DEVIL'S LANGUAGE

The enemy is the greatest liar. John 8:44 (NIV) lets us know why. It says "You belong to your father, the devil, and you want to carry out your father's desires. He was a murderer from the beginning, not holding to the truth, for there is no truth in him. When he lies, he speaks his native language, for he is a liar and the father of lies." Lying is the native language of the enemy. It is the only language he can speak. If he is speaking, it is a lie. His lips do not have the ability to form the truth. If the enemy is speaking to you, just believe the opposite, and that would be the truth.

Lying is the greatest power the enemy has. It is his tool in releasing defeat. He likes to lie to us through circumstances. People, without knowing it, can come into agreement with what the enemy is saying. Oftentimes the enemy begins lying to us when we are children. He will use family members who may have the best intentions, yet they may make statements in agreement with the lie of the enemy, like "you are this," or "you can't succeed at that." Or the situation may make the lie seem obvious to you. It may seem like you're not that smart. You're not that talented. You're not as pretty as someone else. These words and thoughts can go down deep into the heart and soul of a person and begin

45

to shape their self-image. These lies have the potential to paralyze an individual from rising up to their God-given potential.

## VALUE

Everyone loves that wonderful stone called a diamond. What most people don't think about when looking at a diamond is the work that it took to produce it.

Diamonds are made out of carbon — highly organized carbon, that is. Geologists are still guessing how diamonds formed in the Earth from 1 billion to 3 billion years ago, according to a recent study in the journal Nature, but they think the recipe follows something like this:

1. Bury carbon dioxide 100 miles into Earth.
2. Heat to about 2,200 degrees Fahrenheit.
3. Squeeze under pressure of 725,000 pounds per square inch.
4. Quickly rush towards Earth's surface to cool.[17]

The greatness of God inside of us is like a diamond. It sparkles and shines and is highly desirable. The enemy tries to stop it from coming out through his lies. The lies cause us to not want to shine. He does not realize that the pressure he is putting on us is like the pressure and heat the earth puts on a diamond. God will use the pressure in our lives to make us into a diamond. No one wears a coal ring on his or her finger. What is produced after the pressure is what is desirable.

You can drop a diamond in mud and dirt, but it doesn't stop it from being a diamond. One encounter with water will remove all the stuff that covers it. Then it is restored and reveals its true beauty. Covering it up cannot change its value. Your difficult circumstances are like dirt. The lie is that your value is equal to your circumstances. You cannot see your value by looking at your circumstances. You must believe what God says about you.

## THE ENEMY'S PLAN

If we believe lies about ourselves, we will live according to them. We live based on what we see and perceive. We must make sure that we are seeing and perceive the right things, or we will live according to the wrong ones. Are we perceiving what God is saying and doing?

This is the tactic the enemy has used since the beginning. He lied to Adam and Eve. He tried to get them to believe they were not like God even though they already were. The enemy lies to us about our value. If we believe him, we get out of our place. Once we get out of our place, we give up our position of victory. We can't overcome the enemy on his level. We can only overcome from our place of authority, seated with Christ the Victorious One. Seated is the position of victory for a believer. Anything else is playing in the enemy's territory.

Once Eve believed the lie, she responded by living according to the lie. She made choices that came out of the lie. A lie is a seed. When we receive it, a tree of defeat begins to grow. It causes us to produce fruit from the seeds of the lie. These fruits may have different scenarios. But the end result will get us out of our position. Adam and Eve got kicked out of the Garden of Eden because they got out of their position. They believed the lie of the enemy. It led them right out of their position and onto the enemy's playing field of defeat.

We must stop believing lies and believe the truth of the great things that God says about us. Sometimes it is difficult to believe the great things God says about us. We know all of our weakness and downfalls, and it may be hard to see past that. We can be our own worst critics. We can be harder on ourselves than anyone else can. But no matter what our downfalls are, what God says about us is true. God may say you are strong and bold, yet all throughout your life, you might feel timid and weak. Despite your feelings, the truth is you are strong and bold because God said so. The timidity and weakness you have experienced are circumstances that lie to you about who you are. They encourage you to choose to live the lie instead of living the truth of what God says. They are also invitations for you to live the truth!

## DIVINE PERSPECTIVE

Only a divine perspective from God can break through the clutter of lies and cause us to see what God sees in us. Sometimes one of the hardest things to receive is the greatness that God has for us. Below is a famous poem from Marianne Williamson, "A Return to Love."

> Our deepest fear is not that we are inadequate.
> Our deepest fear is that we are powerful beyond measure.
> It is our light, not our darkness that most frightens us ...
> We were born to make manifest the glory of God that
> is within us ...
> And as we let our own light shine, we unconsciously
> give other people permission to do the same ... [18]

When we believe lies about ourselves, we end up shrinking back. We shy away from the brightness God has given us. We become victorious once we choose to believe what God says about us. Victory is knowing who you are in Jesus.

## A LIE IS NOT SELF-SUSTAINING

A lie opposes the truth. It stands against it aggressively. A lie is not self-sustaining. It needs to be defended and protected. Lies must keep protecting themselves from being found out. Lies keep making up stuff to try to keep looking true. I remember as a kid I would lie about something, then get confronted. I then had to come up with another lie to cover the first one.

As a kid, I was not allowed to watch TV until I finished all my homework. However, the cartoons I wanted to watch were the ones that were on when I first came home from school. So I would sneak and watch TV before my mom got home. Then one day she felt the back of the TV when she got home, and the TV was warm from being on all afternoon. She confronted me about it. I think I said "Well it was hot in the house, so maybe the heat got stuck on." So my one lie turned into two lies. Of course, my mom did not believe that.

Lies come to us through our circumstances. These may be the first lie. As we buy into it, the enemy is able to reinforce these lies with more lies by repeating the same kind of circumstances, so that we keep believing it. Lies have a short shelf life. The moment you start to question the lie, it has to repeat itself to convince you again. The first lie will not hold up against you questioning and resisting it.

Rejection is one of those lies. People who struggle with rejection are always thinking about rejection. If I do not feel rejected, the thought of rejection never comes up. The reason they are always thinking about rejection is because it is the lie they have bought. So the enemy keeps repeating the lie to them. The enemy wants to keep that lie in their minds so they keep buying into it. I never think about rejection if I am not rejected. The lie is fighting to stay alive, by always making sure that it is seen and acknowledged. It's agreeing with the lie that gives it a little more lifespan.

Once you choose to stop agreeing with the lie, you now have the power to overcome it. A lie magnifies itself to look bigger than it is. A lie lives in darkness and fear of being found out. It is a house built on stilts. All you have to do is knock over the stilts to bring the whole thing down.

---

[17] Mosher, Dave. "How Are Diamonds Made?" Love Science. November 13, 2012. Accessed July 6, 2016. http://www.livescience.com/32266-how-are-diamonds-made. html.

[18] Williamson, By Marianne. "A Return to Love Quotes by Marianne Williamson." A Return to Love Quotes by Marianne Williamson. Accessed July 10, 2016. https:// www.goodreads.com/work/quotes/1239848-a-return-to-love-reflections-on-the-principles-of-a-course-in-miracles.

# ten

## TRUTH

Truth is a foundation, and it never needs defending. Truth declares who it is without reservation. It speaks boldly and confidently. Truth just stands still. The thought of questioning my name never comes up in my head. I know my name; it's the name that I have had since birth. When someone asks my name, I say it boldly with confidence. I know that someone can't say, "No that is wrong." I know my name, and there is no question about it. The same is true for you, I am sure. No matter where you are or what's going on, your name is the same. You know your name; you know who you are. That is truth.

Truth needs no defending, just like your name. It is established and settled. Your name is what it is and never has to be questioned. I might question something else about myself that is more subjective. The areas where I would question myself would be where I have evidence that shows me something different than I feel. I may feel strong, but then I try to lift something heavy, and it does not move. After that experience, I now have to question my strength. When evidence says something opposite of how I feel, I now am less confident in that area. It causes me to not be as bold and to have doubt in that area.

Once I understand the truth about what God says about that area, I no longer question it. The truth brings confidence.

## TRUTH IS REVEALED

Truth is revealed, not created. Because it is the foundation, it is always there. The truth about gravity will never change. An object will always fall to the ground. Gravity is a truth that God has set as a foundation for life here on earth. That truth of gravity existed before Sir Issac Newton discovered it. The truth of gravity was already in operation, it was just revealed to him. He was able to measure and prove the principle that was already in existence.

Facts changes, but truth does not because it is establish by God. Facts are circumstantial. The fact could be that it's raining right now. In a few minutes that fact may not be true anymore. We can fall into feeling discouraged and stuck when we live out of facts rather than out of truth. For example, we may look at our finances and think, "Man I am poor," and start to live out of the lie of poverty.

## JESUS IS TRUTH

> Jesus saith unto him, I am the way, the truth, and the life: no man cometh unto the Father, but by me. If ye had known me, ye should have known my Father also: and from henceforth ye know him, and have seen him. (John 14:6, 7 KJV)

In John 14:6 Jesus states that he is truth. Truth is not a concept, truth is a person, whose name is Jesus Christ. Jesus is truth!

> "What do you want with us, Jesus of Nazareth ? Have you come to destroy us? I know who you are—the Holy One of God!" "Be quiet!" said Jesus sternly. "Come out of him!" (Mark 1:24-25 NIV)

The unclean spirit spoke accurate words. The words were not truth because they did not come from Jesus, who is truth. If the person of truth did not say it, it is not truth. It may be factually accurate; however, it has to come out of the mouth of the Author of Truth. You can walk into a Louis Vuitton store in a large city in America and buy a bag that was made by them. And you can go online and buy a bag that is not made by them but looks exactly like one of their bags. It has the logo and other matching elements. The fake bag looks like and feels like the real thing, but it will never be the real thing. It can never be the real thing because it was not made by the original designer. No matter how accurate it looks and feels, it's not the truth or the real thing. The source is wrong, so the accuracy of it will still not make it legitimate. Truth is a matter of the source, not the accuracy of details.

We must seek to get the information about ourselves from the right source. Jesus does not posses the ability to lie. If Jesus looks at you and says you are free, then you are free. What he speaks is the truth because he is truth and it is established. It was by that same voice of truth that the earth was formed. When God speaks, creation responds.

Let's look at the following scriptures, with the concept in mind that Jesus is truth.

> Then you will know the truth, and the truth will set you free. (John 8:32 NIV)

Translate it this way: you will know Jesus, and Jesus will set you free.

> Sanctify them by the truth; your word is truth. (John 17:17 NIV)

We are sanctified by Jesus, and Jesus is the word.

Jesus is truth and what he speaks is truth. Jesus speaks his word to us. It is not to inform us or promise us something that is disconnected and separate from himself. He speaks truth to us, which is him declaring himself to us and establishing himself in our lives. In John 1 we see that Jesus and his word are one. Truth is Jesus being established in our lives.

# eleven

## INSECURITIES

We come from different backgrounds culturally, economically and experientially. Millions of things make us different. One thing is the same in us. We all have insecurities. Your insecurities might be different than mine, but we all have insecurities.

Our weakness and insecurities can work against us. Our insecurities can be like the hero in an action movie. No matter how many times it's been shot or blown up, it keeps on finding a way to survive. It keeps on showing up.

An insecurity can just be a way that you feel and think about yourself. You could feel ugly, not smart, less valuable, alone, scared, ashamed. Or there could be a physical defect, a past mistakes, rejection, anger, financial lack, etc. Whether factual or not, these things are different from what God says about us. These areas will cripple our lives if we choose to believe them. A lot of these things can be self-fulfilling prophecies when we try to control them and keep them from happening.

## HOPE IN INSECURITIES

There is hope from being trapped in insecurities:

> But he said to me, "My grace is sufficient for you, for my power is made perfect in weakness." Therefore I will boast all the more gladly about my weaknesses, so that Christ's power may rest on me. (2 Corinthians 12:9 NIV)

Paul shows us the key here. It is to boast in our weakness, not run from it. This may seem counterintuitive to natural human behavior. We would all want to protect ourselves from our weakness, not embrace it.

The word perfect in this passage means to complete. For something to be made complete, all the parts have to be present. A part of his power is to meet the needs of our weakness. It's like a woman's body. She can live without having a child. Once she gets pregnant, her body is designed to meet the needs of creating a baby. God designed us with weakness that he alone is designed to complete. Our weakness is a platform for God's power to be displayed upon.

God is not concerned about our weakness and insecurities. God is secure in his ability to help us overcome our weakness. As we look upon our own weakness, it may seem like the biggest mountain in the world. God sees it as a micro grain of sand in the scope of the universe. We can get frustrated with ourselves when we look at our insecurities. We have to see it through God's abilities and rest in his security.

## OUTSTRETCH YOUR INSECURITIES

Then he went back in the meeting place where he found a man with a crippled hand. The Pharisees had their eyes on Jesus to see if he would heal him, hoping to catch him in a Sabbath infraction. He said to the man with the crippled hand, "Stand here where we can see you." Then he spoke to the people: "What kind of action suits the Sabbath best? Doing good or doing evil? Helping people or leaving them helpless?" No one said a word. He looked them in the eye, one after another, angry now, furious at their hard-nosed religion. He said to the man, "Hold out your hand." He held it out—it was as good as new! The Pharisees got out as fast as they could, sputtering about how they would join forces with Herod's followers and ruin him. (Mark 3:1-5 MSG)

Jesus tells the man with the withered hand "stretch forth your hand." We see no indication that Jesus said stretch forth your withered hand.

He just said stretch out your hand. That man had to choose which hand. He could have stretched out the hand that was fine and shown Jesus his strength: "Look, see Jesus, I am fine. I have no problems." But he knew his only chance of getting his withered hand healed was to not hide it, but rather expose it. He chose to show his weakness and insecurity while everybody in the temple was watching. I am sure there were people there who might not have know he had a withered hand. He was willing to show forth his weakness, and it was then made into a place of strength. The moment he began to show it to Jesus, he got healed.

Ignoring your insecurities will not fix them or cause them to go away. You can never fix something you are not willing to deal with. You have to face them head on. Not dealing with your insecurities can rob you and others of what you have to offer.

## INSECURITIES ROB

Insecurities rob from us if we yield to them. You can be a great singer but have an insecurity about how you sound to others and never sing in public. The gift that God has put inside of you is not being used or shared. You could be afraid to travel because of terrorism or other issues and never see the world. Yielding to our insecurities can rob us of the life Jesus has for us. When I say life, I mean joy and freedom internally and externally. We might be doing ourselves a disservice by not bringing our weakness to Jesus. I have heard it said that pride is the wall that hides our insecurities. When you see someone operating in pride, it's because they are focusing on their strength. They are trying to put their strength on display to cover up their insecurities and weakness. It's saying "Everyone look over here at this great thing I can do, but don't look at this area of weakness."

The vulnerability in our lives puts his strength on display, not our weakness. Vulnerability to God and to people attracts his grace.

Running and hiding from insecurities only keeps us imprison to the defeat. The bondage is that you can't have your weakness exposed or shown. You are bound by the fear of being exposed, so you strive to keep it covered. The key to unlocking the cell is vulnerability. It will set you free to walk in God's sufficient grace and power.

Vulnerability is giving your heart permission to be loved, both in its strength and its weakness, by God. That is freedom.

# twelve

## CONTENDING

con·tend (kən-tĕnd')
v. con·tend·ed, con·tend·ing, con·tends
v.intr.
1. To strive in opposition or against difficulties; struggle: armies contending for control of territory; had to contend with long lines at the airport.
2. To strive in competition, as in a race; vie: two runners contending for the lead.
3. To strive in controversy or debate; dispute.[19]

The word contend lets you know that there is a difficulty. It lets you know that you have to push against some form of resistance. It speaks of a back-and-forth struggle. To me, it means victory is possible.

God has victory and wants to share that victory with us. We live in a natural world and must contend for that victory to be released into our lives. We see in Daniel 10 (NIV) an angel comes to Daniel. He tells Daniel that since the moment he set himself to pray and seek God, his answer was released. Daniel had to contend for it by continuing to fight for twenty-one days in prayer and fasting.

If you have been serving God for more than a year, I am sure you have noticed things don't just become magically easy. We must contend for the victories of God. Something difficult does not mean something is not God or the will of God. We have to contend for what God wants to do.

# DAVID, A MAN OF VICTORY

David said, "I've been a shepherd, tending sheep for my father. Whenever a lion or bear came and took a lamb from the flock, I'd go after it, knock it down, and rescue the lamb. If it turned on me, I'd grab it by the throat, wring its neck, and kill it. Lion or bear, it made no difference—I killed it. And I'll do the same to this Philistine pig who is taunting the troops of God-Alive. God, who delivered me from the teeth of the lion and the claws of the bear, will deliver me from this Philistine." Saul said, "Go. And God help you!" (1 Samuel 17:34-37 MSG)

David was a man of war. He loved victory. David first tasted victory while defending his father's sheep. When a lion and a bear came after the sheep, David protected the sheep and killed both the lion and the bear. He learned to fight in the field. He learned to do whatever was needed to take out the enemy.

From my observation, most soldiers learn to fight before they have to kill. They learn how to punch, shoot, use a sword, etc. David had to kill before he actually had the skill set to fight. David did not care about the art of fighting. He fought to get to the end result, which was a victory over his enemy. We settle for mastering the technique of something and forget about the intended results.

We must become lovers of victory. We must love to see the victory of God over the enemy. The first thing David asks while considering going to fight Goliath was "What do I get when I win?" He had the heart of victory. David had in his mind the end result, which was the reward for taking out Goliath. He knew how to enter a battle with victory in mind.

Like David, we must learn to love victory. Many of us have only tasted defeat. We have had a steady diet of defeat. We have become passive and apathetic. We don't even know how to contend for victory.

I have heard athletes who have come in second place say that they are so hungry for first place. They desire it strongly. They are willing to train with great passion. They know they were so close and had a chance for it. If they fight harder next time, they have a chance to attain first place. The athlete who comes in thirtieth place might just say "Well I gave it a good try. It just did not work out." Victory is so much further than his or her reach that giving up is easier. He or she may not try as hard or be as hungry for it as someone who got closer to it.

David would not have so much confidence to take on Goliath if he had not first taken out the lion and the bear. We have to start where we are at. Look for the little victories first. They will lead to the big ones. Once you get that one taste of victory, you will keep fighting for it, and you will settle for nothing less than it. You will be reconditioned for victory.

The proof of desire is in the pursuit. You can't have victory if you don't desire it. You have to fight for it and press into it. Victory produces victory. A person with a victory mindset has the reward on his or her mind.

## DAVID, A MAN OF WAR

> But God said to me, "You shall not build a house for My name, because you have been a man of war and have shed blood." (1 Chronicles 28:3 NKJV)

David was a man of war. He fought many battles against the enemies of God. He brought forth many victories for God's people. God calls David a man after his own heart. David was not just fighting for himself to get what he wanted. David was after the heart of God. He was fighting to bring forth the will of God. David was contending for the things of God. He brought Heaven to Earth. He was enforcing the victory of God in the world. We are not fighting in the natural, for ourselves or for what we want. We are contending in the spirit to bring forth what God wants now.

We are fighting to see God's victory demonstrated in our lives. Be like David. Get a love for the victory of God. Love to see it released in your life, your family, your church, your community, your city and your nation.

---

[19] "Contend." Dictionary.com. Dictionary.com, n.d. Web. 10 Dec. 2014.

# thirteen

## OBEDIENCE FOR VICTORY

I was invited to attend an event at someone's home who owns several horses. Part of the event was that the host was going to do a horse show for all the guests. He stood in the middle of a beautiful stable in the backyard. The host began to do demonstrations with the horse for us. He gave commands, and the horse acted them out. He made certain sounds and the horse would trot around him. He made other sounds and the horse would walk around him. He had the horse jump small hurdles. He had the horse run, then stop on command. He had the horse walk backward and walk sideways.

That horse did things I did not know were possible for a horse. He said that these were difficult things for a horse to do. It was amazing to watch. He said the key to him bonding with the horse is that he has gained the horses trust. The horse knows he would never hurt him. Then he said that horses are flight animals. If you suddenly scare them, their natural reaction would be to take off running. So he had the horse stand still, and he kept talking to us with the horse standing there. Then when the horse did not expect it, he jumped up and scared the horse. The horse barely responded. The horse took one step back and just looked at the trainer. That horse completely trusted him. He knew that even if something unexpected happened, there was nothing to fear. His master was not going to hurt him, and he is for the horses good.

Through this demonstration, I realized that is what the Lord is trying to teach us. He is trying to get us to be like that horse, fully trusting him and knowing that he has no desire to hurt us. The trust that the horse has in his master is so great that it causes him to defy his natural reflex to run. God wants us to be so yielded to him, like that horse, that our trust in him is greater than our response to the natural things around us. God wants to master us. The trainer who invited us to his house had mastered his horse. He had taken the horse out onto trails that were unfamiliar to him or the horse. These trails had waters, tight trails, and tree trunks blocking the path. He needed the horse to do things that he had never trained the horse to do. The horse completely did it without reservations. The horse was so trusting of the master that he didn't even question what he did not understand. He just completely trusted and obeyed.

Victory is to be like this horse, yielded and submitted to the person of victory, Jesus. Let him guide and lead us into victory. He is the only one who knows the directions to victory. He is our navigation system to victory. Follow his voice, and he will lead you there. Living in a position of victory is simply living connected to the Lord with your heart fully.

## OUR STRENGTHS NOT NEEDED FOR HIS VICTORY

It is human nature to believe that your strengths are your assets. Yet they may be the thing that is holding you back. Don't be limited by your strength. Maybe our real strength is our weakness and dependence on God.

I heard a leadership expert say that he is a great communicator. He said that he would share with his staff great ideas, which they executed well. One day a staff member said to him "You are a great communicator, but your weakness is you don't listen." That caught him by surprise. He then could see how he did not listen to his staff when they had valuable input. He trusted too much in his strength and was not seeing what his weakness was.

To move into victory, we must first realize that we don't have victory. Our strengths look like assets but are actually liabilities in the kingdom if we rely on them for victory. God needs nothing from us. We are chosen by God to fulfill a role not based on any of our strengths, but totally on his.

God wants us to depend on His strength not our own. Zechariah 4:6 (NIV) says "So he said to me, 'This is the word of the LORD to

Zerubbabel: 'Not by might nor by power, but by my Spirit,' says the LORD Almighty." Everything God wants to do will be accomplished by His Spirit, not by us striving in our own ability and strength.

Our potential is far greater than we can ever think or imagine. When we put our trust in God's strength and not our own, we will see it. A little boy had in is had his own strength: five loaves and two fish (John 6:9 NIV) . What was seen as a limitation by so many, Jesus saw as an opportunity for victory to be released. What's in our hands has an exact defined value and potential. It has a far more reaching value when yielded to the Lord.

Victory does not come by performance but by permission from God. He has called us to it. We can't earn it. Victory comes by us yielding to God. That is our fight, to be yielded to Him.

## WE MUST BE ON GOD'S SIDE FOR VICTORY

> Now when Joshua was near Jericho, he looked up and saw a man standing in front of him with a drawn sword in his hand. Joshua went up to him and asked, "Are you for us or for our enemies?" "Neither," he replied, "but as commander of the army of the LORD I have now come." Then Joshua fell facedown to the ground in reverence …
> (Joshua 5:13-14 NIV)

We see in the above scripture that we don't come up with our own teams and expect God to choose if he is on our side. We are the ones that must align with God. Either we are on God's side or we are not. If we expect victory, then we must get on his side. Victory is located on God's side. Victory is the Lord's.

A sailboat's only power is the wind. We must be like a sailboat, put our sail up and depend on the wind of God. We have to trust God however he leads. We embrace our victory by abiding in him. We yield our sails to the Lord to lead us through the open waters of life.

# fourteen

## COMFORT

People desire comfort. No one walks into a mattress store and asks for the hardest and most uncomfortable mattress. We desire physical comfort. We desire emotional comfort. We want to be around people that value us and make us feel safe. That sounds good. Sometimes comfort is not always a good thing though. It becomes a bad thing when we choose comfort over victory.

We can't always have our comfort and God's best for our lives at the same time. What would be our comfort is sometimes contrary to the purpose of God. It is more comfortable to keep your money, but God may be calling you to give it away. God is calling us to live outside of our comfort zone. God wants us to live in his comfort zone, which is walking by his spirit. Our comfort zone is to lead and function out of self-perseveration. We naturally want to be comfortable and want to be in control. God is calling us not to live by the natural but to live by the spirit.

## DON'T TRUST COMFORT

One night I was getting ready to minister at a church. I did not feel settled in my heart about how God was leading me to minister at the service that night. I prayed about it, and I felt the Lord lead me to not follow the notes I had prepared, but to follow what he was doing. I did what I felt the Lord wanted me to do. Later that night I was still not settled about how the ministry time went. I was thinking, "Maybe I did something wrong. Maybe I missed it." So I then began to ask the Lord about it. He responded and said "No, you did what I asked you to do."

I said "Then why do I feel so unsettled and uncomfortable still?" He said "You were being led by my Spirit, and it's uncomfortable to your understanding. In your own understanding, you have nothing to measure your success by." In that moment I had to trust God and not my own ability, that just because I felt uncomfortable did not mean it wasn't God. I had to learn how to get out of my comfort zone.

Living a life of seeking comfort will hinder the work of God in our lives. What is often most comfortable and natural to us will lead us to passivity and apathy. If we follow our own way, it will lead us to death and defeat. God is calling us to live in victory. He is leading us out of our comfort and into his victory.

Jesus rebuked Peter when Peter did not want Jesus to go to the cross. Peter was more concerned with human concerns and life. Once our perspective turns to earthy concerns, we lose our ability to see in the spirit. We get blinded by earthly things. Once our perspective is off, then we will choose the things in this earth to be comfortable. Our comfort zone will lead us to a life of defeat.

## VICTORY MIGHT LOOK DIFFERENT

When I first came to Christian International to go to the Bible college, I had one thought in mind and God had another. The first week of school, we had orientation. One of the staff shared how they came to go to one year of school, but eventually they became staff and had now been there ten years. Another staff member said the same story and had been there for twelve years. Then another said eight years. I thought "Do these people not understand how college works? You leave when you finish school." I said "God that is stupid. That will never be me." Here I am twelve years later, and that is me. God's best for me was to become staff at Christian International. What I thought victory looked like was not what God's victory for me looked like. Never say never to God. He takes it as a personal challenge.

## LIVE BEING CHALLENGED

A caged lion living at the zoo has a comfortable lifestyle. They get food, water to drink, and a little exercise every day. They are created for much more than that. Their bodies are designed for the open plains. The lion functions in his best state when he uses all his abilities to use all the strength that he has. In captivity, he can't run at his full strength. He can only walk around or a mild jog at best. He was meant for more. You are made for more. You are made to live and demonstrate your full strength.

I worked out three times a week for two years and got my body to develop its potential. My strength increased, endurance increased, mobility increased. When I took a break from working out, I lost some of the progress. After a week off from working out, it's hard to start back up. I have no desire to then workout. I get comfortable and don't desire the challenge. In this state, I no longer want to push my body to its full potential. I am missing out on the new strengthen and on the highest my body is capable of. I am not living to my full potential in this state. Yes, it's not always fun to workout, but it is exciting to see what I can do and to function at the greatness that God has for me. We must push for victory.

> And those who belong to Christ Jesus have crucified the
> [a]sinful nature together with its passions and appetites.
> (Galatians 5:24 AMP)

We must be willing to crucify our love for comfort. Loving my comfort more that God can lead us into lives of bondage and defeat. Jesus is true life and freedom. Following him and his way will lead us to victory. We are designed to live a life full of adventure and victory. We are made for the wild, not for a cage. God wants to set you free from the cage and release you into the wild.

# fifteen

## MIGHTY WARRIOR

People picture God as an old man sitting on a throne with a long white beard. They picture a man full of wisdom. They picture a solemn man. This is not at all a biblical view of God. The image that I described is actually Zeus from Greek mythology. Somehow we have let the world influence our view of God through the years. Let's shift our image of God to a strong and mighty warrior ready for battle. He is a strategic warrior with great strength. He chooses a battle plan that destroys the enemy and empowers his children at the same time.

> The LORD your God is with you, the Mighty Warrior who saves. He will take great delight in you; in his love he will no longer rebuke you, but will rejoice over you with singing. (Zephaniah 3:17 NIV)

The Lord is a mighty warrior. *Mighty* is a term that means power or strength. A warrior is someone who is skilled in the area of war or combat. So the Lord identifies himself as a mighty warrior. He is highlighting the fact that he is strong, powerful and skilled in the area of combat. God wants us to understand this part of his nature. He is not afraid of battle. He charges into battle. God leads the charge of victory. I want you to read the following scriptures slowly, and let them paint a picture for you of God as a warrior. Oftentimes we read past scriptures quickly when reading them in a book other than the Bible.

The One who breaks open the way will go up before them; they will break through the gate and go out. Their King will pass through before them, the Lord at their head. (Micah 2:13 NIV)

They will be like mighty warriors in battle,
trampling their enemies in the mud under their feet.
Since the Lord is with them as they fight,
they will overthrow even the enemy's horsemen.
"I will strengthen Judah and save Israel[a];
I will restore them because of my compassion.
It will be as though I had never rejected them,
for I am the Lord their God, who will hear their cries.
The people of Israel[b] will become like mighty warriors,
and their hearts will be made happy as if by wine.
Their children, too, will see it and be glad;
their hearts will rejoice in the Lord.
(Zechariah 10:5-7 NLT)

With God we will gain the victory, and he will trample down our enemies. (Psalm 60:12 NIV)

The LORD will march out like a champion, like a warrior he will stir up his zeal; with a shout he will raise the battle cry and will triumph over his enemies. (Isaiah 42:13 NIV)

But the LORD stands beside me like a great warrior. Before him my persecutors will stumble. They cannot defeat me. They will fail and be thoroughly humiliated. Their dishonor will never be forgotten. (Jeremiah 20:11 NLT)

The LORD will march forth like a mighty hero; he will come out like a warrior, full of fury. He will shout his battle cry and crush all his enemies. (Isaiah 42:13 NLT)

These are just a few scriptures that describe God's nature as a warrior. I decided to leave out some for the sake of space in this book and did not list every scripture I could find that describes him as a warrior. As we read through the Old Testament, we see God lead His people into battle after battle. We see that God was with them and gave them the victory over their enemies. God did not send them to war and then turn his head away and say "Let me know when it's done." No, God ran to the battle with them and fought with them and through them to bring forth his kingdom and purpose. God is a mighty warrior who loves his victory.

> As they fled before Israel on the road down from Beth Horon to Azekah, the LORD hurled large hailstones down on them, and more of them died from the hail than were killed by the swords of the Israelites. (Joshua 10:11 NIV)

We see in this scripture God threw hailstones down at the enemy. God fought alongside Israel. He is experienced in war because he gets involved in the war.

## WWI ANGELS

We see throughout scripture that God fought for Israel. I want to share with you an event that happened in World War I where God fought for his purposes. I want to share with you an excerpt from an article from Steve Collins about a battle that happened on August 26, 1924:

> It took place when the German Army was on the offensive and advancing against the allied French and English armies. It was early in World War I, and there was then only a small British Expeditionary Force (BEF) fighting alongside the French army. During a battle fought near Mons, Belgium, the French army retreated and the small British force took the brunt of the advancing Germans. The article in Military Heritage states that "The odds

were 4-to-1 against the BEF in infantry, plus the usual German superiority in guns." Although the British fought bravely as they attempted an orderly retreat in the face of superior numbers, they finally reached the point where "the Germans were coming on in such overwhelming numbers that rifles and courage could not hold them any longer." Then, according to many witnesses who were actually participants in the battle, a miracle occurred. The angels came.

The article contains numerous, first-hand accounts of British soldiers who witnessed the events that day. Some angels were described as a "shadowy army...of bowmen," and other British soldiers witnessed "unearthly figures materialize ... above the German lines. They were winged like angels." There were accounts that the angelic army was led by a "tall, yellow-haired man on a white horse, wearing golden armor and wielding a sword." There were reports of hails of arrows being unleashed by the angelic bowmen which "cut down the enemy en masse." According to the article, "the German General Staff [found] the bodies of hundreds of their men lying on the battlefield with no discernible wounds..." It was not only common foot soldiers who saw the angels, but NCOs and officers did as well. A British colonel is quoted as saying "...the thing happened. You need not be incredulous. I saw it myself." The article also mentions a confirming account by a Captain Hayward, an intelligence officer with British I Corps who saw "four or five wonderful beings" and "figures of luminous beings." The article also cites confirming evidence by German prisoners in the battle who also saw the angels.[20]

This account from modern history is similar to accounts we see in scripture. It reminds me of when the prophet Elijah prayed God would open his servants eyes to see the angels that were on their side (2 Kings

6:6). The Lord is not far from our human situations. God is right in the middle of them. He fights for his purpose in and through our lives. When God steps onto a battlefield, he fights to win, and victory is inevitable. He is a victorious warrior.

## YOU ARE A MIGHT WARRIOR

> When the angel of the LORD appeared to Gideon, he said, "The LORD is with you, mighty warrior." (Judges 6:12 NIV)

The Lord is a mighty warrior, but he has also called us to be mighty warriors for him. God wants our agreement here on earth. God wants us to be willing to fight for his victory to come forth in the earth. God has called us to be warriors for him. We are part of the army of the Lord. He is the Mighty Warrior leading his troops of mighty warriors into a victorious battle.

## MANTLED WITH VICTORY

> In the year that King Uzziah died, I saw the Lord, high and exalted, seated on a throne; and the train of his robe filled the temple. (Isaiah 6:1 NIV)

In the above scripture, Isaiah has a vision of the Lord high and lifted up. He then describes what the Lord is wearing. He said the train of his robe filled the temple. During that time in history, kings would wear ornate robes. It represented their majesty and authority. The longer the train, which was the back hem of the robe, the more powerful the king. The train was the part of the king's garment that extended behind the king. After a king defeated an army in battle, he would cut off a portion of the defeated king's robe. He would then have it sewn onto his own train. The length of a king's robe showed the number of victories he had.

God is mantled in victory. His victories filled the temple. That speaks to the fact the he has won so many battles that the victory has filled his house. I believe each one of us is a part of that victory. He has won the victory of our lives. He won us from the enemy. God is full of victory. He wears victory as a garment. He is a mighty warrior with a track record of victory to prove it.

---

[20] Collins, Steven. "THE DAY THE ANGELS SAVED THE BRITISH ARMY." Prophecy Updates and Commentary. 2009. Accessed August 16, 2016. http://stevenmcollins.com/WordPress/the-day-the-angels-saved-the-british-army/.

# sixteen

## ROYALTY

Royal:

adjective

1.of or relating to a king, queen, or other sovereign:
royal power; a royal palace.

2.descended from or related to a king or line of kings:
a royal prince.

3. noting or having the rank of a king or queen.

4. established or chartered by or existing under the patronage of a sovereign:
a royal society.

5. (*initial capital letter*) serving or subject to a king, queen, or other sovereign.

6. proceeding from or performed by a sovereign:
a royal warrant.

7. appropriate to or befitting a sovereign; magnificent; stately:
royal splendor.

But you are not like that, for you are a chosen people. You are royal priests, a holy nation, God's very own possession. As a result, you can show others the goodness of God, for he called you out of the darkness into his wonderful light. (1 Peter 2:9 NLT)

In the above scripture, God calls us royal. We are not what we think about ourselves. We are not what our circumstances say we are. We are what God declares about us. If God says we are royal, then we are royal. In Revelations 19:16 it says that he is king of kings. He rules over every king. He has the greatest authority over all. God has called us a royal priesthood. We are called into God's royalty.

## DUTIES OF ROYALTY

Being royalty comes with a certain mindset and duties that must be fulfilled. A royal person does not operate like everyone else in the territory. They can't walk by and see something wrong in the territory and not doing anything about it. They are responsible for governing the kingdom. Everything is under their authority. Anything that is is out of place reflects on them because they are the governor of things. It would be irresponsible for a person of royalty to not attend to the needs of what is under their leadership.

Royalty takes responsibility for what is wrong even if it's not your fault. God is the King of Kings. He came down and died for us. He is royalty. He came down to love and rescue us. Our sin was not his fault, but he was willing to take our sins. God stepped in and used his authority to impact our lives.

We are called, as God demonstrated, to use the authority we have been given to make an impact in the world around us. We need a mindset of taking responsibility for things that need to change. We can become the solution needed. We have a royal duty to take responsibility. God has placed things under our care and authority.

## THE FIRSTBORN OF ROYALTY

The firstborn child in a royal family is next in line for the throne. That child has all the responsibility placed on their shoulders. They are who everyone is looking at to see how they carry themselves and treat people. The firstborn sets the standard, and the other kids follow the older sibling's leadership.

Jesus is the firstborn of many brethren. Romans 8:29 (NIV)says "For those God foreknew he also predestined to be conformed to the image of his Son, that he might be the firstborn among many brothers and sisters."

He is the firstborn, the one that leads the way before us. We don't have to re-invent the wheel, only follow the path that he has set for us. As we read through the gospels, we see his blueprint. All that is left behind him is victory and a defeated enemy. Even when things were not easy for Jesus, victory was always his outcome.

I did not have any older siblings; however, I did have lots of older cousins. Kids would often say taunting things to me. Then I would have a big bold response to them. I knew I had someone bigger on my side who would help me when I backed myself into a corner that I could not get out of on my own. I did not feel afraid or threatened. I knew I had my two older cousins attending the same school and knew they were close by. I remember once running home from school after having too big of a mouth. My mouth got me into a lot of trouble. I did not have the physical ability to defend from the trouble I got myself in. This time, I was not able to find my cousins at school, so I had to run home while a group of about five boys chased me. The way to survive in school in the Bronx was either you were pretty tough or you ran fast. I opted for running fast.

You become a lot bolder when you have someone strong on your side. You don't run from a fight, you run towards a fight, because you know victory is assured. If you go to a knife fight driving a tank, you enter pretty confidently. The reason is you have the superior strength on your side. People only run from the fight they are not sure they can win.

## FAMILY PRIVILEGES

Having predestinated us unto the adoption of children
by Jesus Christ to himself, according to the good pleasure
of his will. (Ephesians 1:5 NIV)

We have been adopted into the family of God. As believers we are adopted into the family of God, and Jesus becomes our elder brother, who is fighting for us.

It would be a great opportunity to do business with Bill Gates and Warren Buffet. They are two of the wealthiest people in the world. It would be great to be the person from whom Bill Gates bought a house, or even to be the real estate agent. The commission on that real estate check would be great. Yet there is something better than getting to do business with these men. What if you found out that Bill Gates and Warren Buffet were your older brothers. That would be so exciting. You would now get to interact with them on a regular basis: at family reunions, weddings, holiday functions. They are now within reach and accessible. This is greater than being able to do business with them, whether one time or even on a regular basis. You now can get to know them. Having this new position with them also means having access to their resources. It's not about the things these men have: money, houses, airplanes, etc. It's about who they are that gives them great influence and creates access to great resources. With Warren Buffet, you are getting decades of amazing insight into business. With Bill Gates, you are getting insight into technology. Having access to them is greater than just having access to their stuff.

At one time Oprah discovered that she found her long lost younger sister. Oprah paid for her sister's education and bought her a house. Oprah just recently met her sister. Based on her default relationship of being sisters, she wanted the best for her sister. She helped her get to a better place in life through the resources that she possessed.

Jesus is our elder brother and he is within reach. We have access to him because he is family. Having access to him, we get his resources by relating to him continually. We don't relate to get things from him, but because we relate to him and he is near, all that he is becomes near to us also. Jesus is the victory over sickness, poverty, disappointment, failure, sorrow, loss, broken heartedness, etc. Jesus, the elder brother on your side, changes everything.

## GOD IS ON YOUR SIDE

We are to follow the path set before us by our elder brother into victory. When we stay closely connected to his heart, we can expect victory. Our elder brother is victorious. Our elder brother is on your side and he is fighting for you.

For a long time, you have been used to protecting and standing up for yourself. You have thought "there is no one else that will do this for me if I don't." The lie of the enemy against you has been that you have to do this on you own. God says, "I am setting you free from that lie. I am on your side. I am here, not just here, but here for you. I am for you, not against you. Come under my wing, and I will take care of you. You don't have to fight to protect yourself or defend yourself anymore. I am your protector. I am your defender,. Let me draw close to you. Are you willing to put things in my hands and let me be your elder brother and take care of you?"

# seventeen

## JERICHO

Now the gates of Jericho were securely barred because
of the Israelites. No one went out and no one came in.
(Joshua 6:6 NIV)

Let us take a look at the story from Joshua 6. If you have spent any time
around Christianity, you know this story.

Then the Lord said to Joshua, "See, I have delivered
Jericho into your hands, along with its king and its
fighting men. March around the city once with all the
armed men. Do this for six days. Have seven priests
carry trumpets of rams' horns in front of the ark. On
the seventh day, march around the city seven times,
with the priests blowing the trumpets. When you hear
them sound a long blast on the trumpets, have the whole
army give a loud shout; then the wall of the city will
collapse and the army will go up, everyone straight in.". . .
The seventh time around, when the priests sounded the
trumpet blast, Joshua commanded the army, "Shout! For
the Lord has given you the city!. . . When the trumpets
sounded, the army shouted, and at the sound of the
trumpet, when the men gave a loud shout, the wall
collapsed; so everyone charged straight in, and they took
the city. (Joshua 6:2-20 NIV)

So from this text we see that Jericho was a walled city. They were on lock down, nothing coming in or going out. I am sure they had every exit and entrance covered with soldiers. Doors and windows would be barricaded. They did everything they could to keep intruders out.

A customary battle strategy in that situation is to bring a battering ram. It's used to continually ram on the main entrance until it breaks down. The other strategy was to get several wooden ladders and place them on the wall to send troops over the wall. I am sure Jericho had all their defenses set in preparation for these strategies. They probably had all their troops lined inside the compound ready to brace the main entrance. The would have been expecting Joshua's men to start ramming the fortress door. I am sure they had people ready on the walls to push ladders off, light them on fire, etc.

God gave Joshua the strategy to fight this battle. This was different than conventional tools of warfare. I am sure once they started to march around the city, the people of Jericho were confused. How is this going to work? This strategy confused both Jericho and Israel.

The people in the city could have been yelling insults. They could have been throwing things and had weapons pointed at the Israelites. It was most likely a hostile environment. Israel had to trust God in the face of hearing these insults and mockery. They had to not get discouraged or give up on what seemed like a ridiculous battle strategy.

The people had to march around the walls seven times before they could shout. I believe every lap around that walled city was removing the defeat from inside of them and building faith. With each step that they took, they had to trust God that this was the right choice to make.

## THE STRATEGY

The priests were also sent to march and blow trumpets, while the people marched around in silence. The trumpets represented the voice of the Lord. While they were marching in silence, God was not silent. God was speaking to them. God told Joshua to march around six times in silence, and then on the seventh time they were to shout. The walls did not come down in the six silent marches, but rather on the seventh with the sound of victory, which is a shout.

Finally on the final day and lap around, they were able to shout, and the walls of the city came falling down. When the walls fell, I'm sure the soldiers of Jericho did not expect that. They were not prepared for that plan of attack. They were most likely shocked and now too full of fear to even respond with a defensive effort. The wall crumbling to the ground possibly killed most of Jericho's fighters. They were prepared to defend and attack over the walk or the main entrance. The Israelites would have been able to go in and completely destroy Jericho. They most likely had little to no resistance.

What seemed impossible to bring down came down with the shout of God. How is it possible for one shout to do this?

## POWER OF A SHOUT

The shout that the Israelites released at Jericho was not just raising their voices to a high decimal level. The shout was full of a lot more than that. This is what the Matthew Henry commentary says about their shout:

> This was a shout of faith; they believed that the walls of Jericho would fall, and by this faith, the walls were thrown down. It was a shot of prayer, an echo to the sound of the trumpets which proclaimed the promise that God would remember them; with one accord, as one man, they cry to heaven for help, and help comes in.[21]

This shout was full of faith, and it was their hearts in agreement with the heart of God. They made an appeal to Heaven. This was their voices on earth joining with God's voice in Heaven. It was making one sound that brought Heaven to earth. Heaven showed up at Jericho and shifted things for the purposes of God. Jericho only had one outcome left, and that was to be defeated because victory was now present. The people's hearts became full of victory.

This shout tells every resistance inside of you to shut up and submit to what God says is possible. In that moment, you let go of every fear, every insecurity, every doubt. You step out of the boat of your comfort, and you meet him standing on the water of your impossibility. Everything changes in that moment. I have seen this shout in action. I have seen people get healed in their bodies. I have seen people get deliverance in that moment. I have seen people break out of depression. It is amazingly powerful when Heaven and earth meet in the place of the shout.

## THE WEAPON OF THE SHOUT

The greatest weapon of power the church has is the shout. God arises in the shouts of his people. It is like an atomic bomb in the spirit that blasts everything of the enemy away. - Bishop Bill Hamon[22]

A few years ago I was invited to speak at a youth conference in Gainesville, Florida. When I got up and started to speak, it was a difficult atmosphere. The young people were disengaged. It felt like I was talking to a wall. Granted they were not used to the subject matter I was speaking on. I was teaching on the prophetic. It just would not break through and connect. I started to ask the Lord in that moment what was going on, and what did I need to do. I felt the Lord say that they were so bound by defeat, they could not break out to receive the teaching. Then I felt like the Lord said to have them shout. I thought, "Well they already are not responsive, they will not shout I am sure." So I had them all stand up and shout. Some did not respond. I started to lead them, saying we are not moving on until I have 100% audience participation. So I kept pushing them. Some gave a little "aha" while others were fully engaged. We kept going until everyone was pushing in. I said "Keep shouting until whatever is holding you back breaks off of you." Then something happened. Shouts started to turn to screams. People started to weep uncontrollably. People started to shake and fall out. People started running around the room. People started to come to the front and lay at the altar weeping. Whether they wanted to shout at first or not, God used that shout to start to set them free.

# SHOUTING BREAKS THE NORMAL

In the natural, we shout when we see a victory, like when an Olympic athlete breaks a world record. In the kingdom, we can shout before we see the walls come down because our shout will cause the walls to come down. Joshua and the children of Israel caused the victory to come by shouting.

A shout is one of God's tools to get us to step out of ourselves and do something we don't normally do in our day-to-day lives. A shout requires us to use one of our most important assets, our voice. It is through our voice that we speak and reveal what is in our hearts. It is the main way we connect with each other. A shout demands that we take this most precious asset and push it to the extreme. The act of shouting requires us to take our voices to the furthest extent they can possibly go. Shouting risks that we can lose it all together. In a shout you're saying to God, "Take me to my limit. Take me to the end of myself and what is possible for me to the place where you begin."

We live our daily lives, for the most part, at a monotone level. The conversations we have in our daily interactions are at a monotone level. It only changes when we are upset or excited about something. Nothing in the average daily life causes us to break through the monotone level.

Victory is at a shout, louder than your normal day-to-day life. Victory is a step higher than where most of us are living. You talk to your friends at a certain level. You work at a certain level. The only things that are at a different level of volume is celebration or devastation. You may have a surprise party for someone. Everyone hides, then yells "surprise," and that is at a different volume than your day-to-day life. The other is the loud sobs of a tragic event or difficult situation.

## A MODERN EXAMPLE OF THE POWER OF THE SHOUT

Bishop Bill Hamon was in Mexico ministering. He was teaching that God wants to fight for you. He taught from Joshua 10:11 (NIV). Its says this:

As they fled before Israel on the road down from Beth
Horon to Azekah, the Lord hurled large hailstones down
on them, and more of them died from the hail than were
killed by the swords of the Israelites.

He used the example of God throwing hailstones at the enemies. At
the end of the message, he led the people in a shout to agree that God
was fighting for them. As they began to shout, it began to hail outside,
which was nowhere in the forecast. Below is the news story.

A hailstorm of mammoth proportions hammered
sections of Mexico City Sunday. Several feet of hail
piled up, making some city roads impassable.

"Roads such as the North Loop [el Periférico Norte]
were flooded by hail and flooding, so municipal and
Federal District workers labored for hours to clear them,
Notimex reported," wrote CNN Mexico. Mexico news
organization Azteca Noticias called it a "historical
hailstorm".[23]

This was a demonstration of God confirming his desire to fight for
and with us. There is another story of Bishop Bill Hamon leading the
people in a shout similar to this in Columbia. This time he led them to
release a shout believing God to help stop the main drug cartel in that
area. They did that should. Within the next forty-eight hours, that cartel
leader who had been at large for a long time was caught. The shout is a
powerful weapon to release God's victory.

## SHOUTING SETS YOU FREE

Have you ever seen that person who always talks too loudly no matter
the setting? Usually, they are always being told to talk softer. Culture and
society are always trying to say "don't stand out but conform." That kind
of thinking keeps you in defeat. If you begin to rise above the monotone,
you may get praise or you may get criticized. Your greatest critics, once

you start moving to a place of victory, will be those who have given up. You arising is exposing to them areas where they have given up. They have taken up residence in defeat, and they want to have company and not be left alone there.

The volume of victory is loud. A football team that just won the Super Bowl does not give a golf clap. They shout until their throats hurt. Passivity will always put the finger to the lips and say "ssshhh, that's not needed."

Shouting also brings internal walls down. In the natural, shouting has several benefits. It opens up blocked memories. A shout helps physical pain to be released from the body. Arthur Janov, Ph.D. developed what is called Primal Therapy. It is a type of therapy in which you don't sit and talk about what you have experienced. You scream and shout. This process helps to release trauma that a person has gone through. It unblocks memories they don't remember. Testimonies have come from it. People's bodies have been healed after they go through this. It releases childhood hurts and pains that people have kept locked up inside, which otherwise would lead to self-destructive behaviors.[24]

God uses the shout to bring deliverance to us and to heal our hearts and emotions. The shout brings his victory into us and causes the attacks of the enemy to flee from us.

Victory is a shout!

---

[21] "Joshua 6 Commentary - Matthew Henry Commentary on the Whole Bible (Complete)." Bible Study Tools. Accessed May 20, 2016. http://www.biblestudytools.com/commentaries/matthew-henry-complete/joshua/6.html.

[22] citation for Bishop's quote

[23] Service, Forecast National Weather. "Two to Three Feet of Hail Crippled Parts of Mexico City Sunday." Washington Post. August 19, 2014. Accessed August 10, 2016. https://www.washingtonpost.com/news/capital-weather-gang/wp/2014/08/19/two-to-three-feet-of-hail-crippled-parts-of-mexico-city-sunday/.

[24] "Primal Therapy." Wikipedia. Accessed November/December, 2015. https://en.wikipedia.org/wiki/Primal_therapy.

# eighteen

## COME OUT OF HIDING

More than we want victory for ourselves, God wants victory for us. God's heart is for us to experience victory. John 10:10 (NKJV) says God wants to give us abundant life. You could also describe abundant life as a victorious life. God does not want us defeated and discouraged. He wants us victorious. God is calling us to come into victory.

Sometimes it is hard to come out of hiding when hiding is familiar to us. I love the song "Out of Hiding" written by Steffany Gretzinger and Amanda Cook. It expresses God's calling to come to that place of victory. God has made the way for us, and he is telling us that it's okay, we can follow after to him.

Here is a portion of the lyrics to "Out of Hiding":

> Out of Hiding
> By Amanda Cook and Steffany Gretzinger
> Come out of hiding, you're safe here with Me …
> You've been on lockdown and I hold your key
> 'Cause I loved you before you knew what was love …
> Now rid of the shackles, My victory's yours …
> There's no reason to stand at a distance anymore …
> No need to be frightened by intimacy
> Just throw off your fear and come running to me …
> © 2014 Bethel Music Publishing
> CCLI Song #7029057[25]

These lyrics paint a beautiful picture of God calling us to come to him. We are not waiting on God to bring victory to us. God is waiting for us to come into his victory. It's like we have theses chains on and are trying to get them off by ourselves, and God says "I have the key, so come to me." It's silly to struggle with the chains when he has the key. God's victory is ours.

## RUN THROUGH THE MINEFIELD

Our natural instinct when we get hurt is to pull back. We run to caves and we look out at the world through the rock. We look to see if we can still see the perceived danger out there. We may view outside the cave as a minefield. Each step we take is filled with fear and resistance, and if we take the wrong step, we fear we will step on a land mine and blow up. None of us wants to experience hurt or pain. We try to avoid it, and that is instinctual. You don't see a rusted nail sitting straight up and choose to step on it barefoot. You avoid it. God wants us to run out of our confined caves and into the open place.

I have heard my mentor Prophet Bill Lackie say that the wall you build to protect yourself from pain is the same wall that also keeps God out. Once you build a wall or run into a cave, it does not discriminate. It keeps the good and the bad out. It isolates you and separates you from getting the healing that is needed. God is calling us out of our caves, through the minefields.

Are you willing to run through your perceived minefields to get to him? More than anything we have populated the minefield more in our minds than it actually is. We have built it up with hurts and pains that we have gone through. God is calling us out to let us know that it's not that bad out there. It truly is an open field with beautiful flowers ready to be run through with open arms. It's like the scene in "Sound of Music" where Julie Andrews is singing and spinning care-free in the meadow.

## GOD CALLS US TO VICTORY

God calls us to victory. He is drawing us out of our caves of defeat. We have to learn that victory is for us. We have experienced defeat. It's now time to experience victory. God is drawing us out of the darkness of defeat into the open fields of light and victory.

He moved away from there and dug another well, and they did not quarrel over that one; so he named it Rehoboth (broad places), saying, "For now the Lord has made [a]room for us, and we shall be [b]prosperous in the land." (Genesis 26:22 AMP)

Like Issac, we have to abandon the cave. We must run into Rehoboth, the open space that God has created for us to prosper. God made this place for us. It is his desire for us to move into this open space. He calls us to leave the confined cave and move into the land of open victory. Victory is desired for us by God. He is leading us into it. We must lay down our defeat mentality to take up a victory mentality. To do this we must leave the caves. Will you let him lead you into victory?

---

[25] By Amanda Cook and Steffany Gretzinger. "Coming out of Hiding (a Reprise)." In My Fathers House. February 13, 2016. Accessed June 13, 2016. https://melwild. wordpress.com/2016/02/13/coming-out-of-hiding-a-reprise/.

# nineteen

## GET STRONGER

Saved or not saved, when a crisis happens, people cry out to God. They pray asking God to immediately fix their situation. They want whatever the crisis is to stop. We often want our situation to change right away, to stop us from being uncomfortable. God has another view about what we see as something we need fixed right away. While we are crying out for things around us to change, God sees an opportunity for us to change. Sometimes God calms the storm, but more often he calms us.

God wants to change us more than he wants to change our situation and circumstance. Bishop Bill Hamon says "God can bring people, places and resources at any time, but he can't give you wisdom and maturity over night." We want to run to the end result when God wants to mature us for the end result.

When you go through tough things, it makes you stronger. Anyone that you talk to that has accomplished anything significant has also gone through hard things. The hard things they went through made them tough to be able to do the things that have never been done. Tough times will produce amazing results. Robert Schuller has a book called *Tough Times Never Last, But Tough People Do!* I think that statement speaks for itself. Whatever did not kill you made you stronger. It's like working out. It is tiring and hurts, but when you are done, you have muscles you did not have before.

## PROCESSED FOR THE MOUNTAIN TOP

There is something called altitude sickness:

> Altitude sickness occurs when you cannot get enough oxygen from the air at high altitudes. This causes symptoms such as a headache, loss of appetite, and trouble sleeping. It happens most often when people who are not used to high altitudes go quickly from lower altitudes to 8000 ft (2438 m) or higher.[26]

Here is the most extreme scenario. Take someone who lives at the lowest land mass on earth, such as the Dead Sea shore at -413 meters (-1354.9 feet). Fly them to highest land mass on earth, Mt. Everest at 8,850 meters (29,035 feet). That person would for sure have some altitude sickness. Those two extreme differences would be such a shock to his or her system.

The way you are able to survive at that extreme altitude change, from the Dead Sea shore to Mt. Everest, is by transitioning slowly. You slowly move to a higher altitude and let your lungs adjust. You can't make that jump overnight. The slow process is necessary so you can survive at the mountain top.

The process you go through to acclimate for the mountain top is the skill set you will need to be sustained there. You can't skip the process and expect to be successful on the mountain top. The process prepares you for the mountain top. If you get dropped off by a helicopter on Mt. Everest from the shore of the Dead Sea, you will never make it.

God wants to teach you to climb the mountain so that you can rule the mountain. God is preparing his people to be able to stand on mountain tops and be able to breathe normally. God does not want us to get to the mountain tops and be gasping for air. He wants us to have gone through the process and have been acclimated to where he takes us.

## MADE READY FOR VICTORY

We may wonder why we don't see a breakthrough we have been believing for. It's not always the enemy. Sometimes God is the one resisting us because we are not ready for the breakthrough. You would never give the keys to a Rolls Royce to a nine-year-old and say "go have fun." That nine-year-old is not ready for it. It's way more than they can handle.

> And I will send hornets before you, which shall drive out the Hivite, the Canaanite, and the Hittite from before you. I will not drive them out from before you in one year, lest the land become desolate and the beasts of the field become too numerous for you. Little by little I will drive them out from before you, until you have increased, and you inherit the land. (Exodus 23:28-30 NKJV)

In the above scripture, God tells Israel they were not ready to handle all the land. They didn't have enough people to manage it. That land would overtake them. It would be like having one person responsible for picking up trash for all the United States. There is no way they could manage all that alone. God wants us to be establish and matured in the things he provides. If we get what we want, when we want it, but are not ready for it, it will do us more harm than good.

## MANAGING VICTORY

Victory comes with responsibilities of its own. You have to learn how to manage the victory you have. The fear of success can also be a limitation to us. It may be easy to believe that you have the potential to succeed. It is another matter altogether to actually succeed. We don't often talk about the challenges that come with success.

Sometimes we do not receive the victory of Jesus because we are afraid of succeeding. We don't want to be responsible for it. Taking on the responsibility of success will force us out of our comfort zone. It will move us from being stuck to being in motion. As you move into new areas of success, you gain a lot more responsibility. There is a demand to engage life at a higher level.

If a company quickly grows beyond its infrastructure, it can't manage that increase. What would happen if a product from a small home company were to get national exposure suddenly? Let's say a celebrity mentions it on social media and the product is now in high demand. Let's assume the home company can make ten of those products by hand an hour. But they get an order for 100,000 units of the product. It will take them 10,000 hours around the clock to fulfill that order. That is 416 days. It will take them over a year to fulfill the order. Success at that rate of speed has the ability to actually destroy the business.

They would have to adapt quickly. Now they would have to figure how to make the products faster. They would need to find a bigger space to produce the products. They'd have to hire more staff. They now have a larger volume of everything to manage. If the structure of the business already had cracks at a smaller level, at this level those cracks have the ability to completely spit wide open.

Success and victory are heavy. Let God make you strong enough to bear it well. This is also one reason people run away from it. Not rising up to it will benefit no one. God is making you strong to carry the greatness he has called you to.

---

[26] "Altitude Sickness-Topic Overview." WebMD. Accessed August 17, 2016. http://www. webmd.com/a-to-z-guides/tc/altitude-sickness-topic-overview#1.

# twenty

## THE VOICE OF THE LORD
## RELEASES VICTORY

The voice of the Lord is over the waters;
the God of glory thunders,
the Lord thunders over the mighty waters.
The voice of the Lord is powerful;
the voice of the Lord is majestic.
The voice of the Lord breaks the cedars;
the Lord breaks in pieces the cedars of Lebanon.
He makes Lebanon leap like a calf,
Sirion[a] like a young wild ox.
The voice of the Lord strikes
with flashes of lightning.
The voice of the Lord shakes the desert;
the Lord shakes the Desert of Kadesh.
The voice of the Lord twists the oaks[b]
and strips the forests bare.
And in his temple all cry, "Glory!"
Psalm 29:3-9(NIV)

We see in the scripture above what the voice of the Lord is capable of doing. The voice of the Lord has potential to change everything. In verse number five, it says the voice of the Lord breaks in pieces the cedars of Lebanon. The cedars of Lebanon were strong trees. They were not easily broken. According to Wikipedia the cedars of Lebanon

(Cedrus libani) can grow to 130 feet tall and eight feet, two inches in diameter.[27]

This wood is used to build ships and used to build temples. The voice of the Lord easily breaks and destroys the strongest of wood. This verse speaks of the strength in the Lord's voice. In Isaiah 2:13 (NKJV) the cedars of Lebanon were used to represent the pride of man. The voice of the Lord destroys the pride of man also. The voice of the Lord can quickly deflate our puffed up strength.

## CREATION IN THE VOICE

In Genesis 1, God speaks and things are created. God's voice has creative power to it. We speak to each other to exchange information. Our words communicate our thoughts, heart, intellect, ideas. When God speaks, something happens. His words do not just communicate. His words create. His words are powerful. They carry in them everything needed to fulfill them.

> So will My word be which goes out of My mouth;
> It will not return to Me void (useless, without result),
> Without accomplishing what I desire, And without succeeding in the matter for which I sent it. (Isaiah 55:11 AMP)

God's voice will do the purpose for which God spoke it out of his mouth. His word is like a seed. In a seed is a whole tree. Once the seed it planted, it can grow and produce a tree. That tree can produce fruit. That fruit will produce seeds. Those seeds can be planted and produce more trees. Those trees can reproduce the whole process. One word from God can produce perpetually.

## VIE MAGAZINE

I want to share a story with you about a women named Lisa Burwell, who is a part of Vision Church @ Christian International where my wife and I attend. She and her husband owned a successful advertisement firm in our area. Almost every major business account in our area came through her office. They were the go-to company to make your mark and impact in our area. They were good at what they did. Then the economic crisis of 2007-2008 hit. Most of their major clients had to pull back on advertising. Those companies had to cut their advertising budget down to nothing. Most of her business was drying up. Like most American small businesses during that time, she was in a tight place.

They were struggling to keep the lights on and pay the staff. Some tough choices had to be made. In this place of uncertainty, she began to pray. She said, "God, I have committed my business to you. What do you want me to do? Do I need to change something; do I close this all down?"

Then the Lord said to her "I want you to start a magazine and name the magazine 'V.'" She said "What Lord? Maybe you don't understand my situation. I don't have any money. I don't know anything about doing a magazine. How am I to start something new, when I am at the end of something that was successful?" Then Lisa said, "Okay God, if that's what you want."

A magazine with the name of a letter did not make much sense to her. She began to flip through the dictionary, looking up words that started with V. None of the words she saw made any sense, until she came across this three letter word "VIE." In french, it's the word for *life*. God was speaking life into her dying business. Lisa obeyed God and launched out in this new territory that did not seem to make logical sense.

Today VIE Magazine has become a thriving magazine in the southeast since it launched in 2008. It has been in disturbed in national chains such as Barnes & Nobel, Books-A-Million, Rite Aid, and more than 150 bookstores throughout the country. After three years in publication, VIE was displayed in lights on a 7,400 square-foot digital board in Time Square, the heart of New York City. One and a half million New Yorkers were exposed to this magazine that God spoke into existence.[28]

I was once on a flight heading home and looked over and saw someone reading VIE Magazine. It made me think about how the person reading that magazine has no idea the backstory of this magazine coming into existence. All of this came out of one woman being brave enough to listen to God speak an answer to her situation.

The voice of the Lord brought victory. God always has something to say about your situation. God wants to speak and release life into whatever you're facing. God has a strategy for victory for you.

## THINGS CHANGE WHEN GOD SPEAKS

When God speaks, a situation changes. God's voice is the deciding factor when something is difficult or looks impossible. We can see countless examples of this throughout scripture. When God speaks it brings victory to people and situations. When God speaks it produces results that bring impact.

The voice of the Lord can quickly shift you into victory. God spoke to Lisa Burwell and shifted her into a place of victory. God wants to release answers to you and shift you into victory. Are you asking and listening to the answers that God is speaking to you?

## LET GOD SPEAK TO YOU

> My sheep hear My voice, and I know them, and they
> follow Me. (John 10:27 NASB)

God wants to release his voice of victory to you. God wants to speak to you and bring answers from Heaven to what you are facing. Give him a place to speak to you.

## THREE STEPS TO HEAR FROM GOD

1. Take time to pray and ask God to speak to you.
2. Wait for God to speak to you.
3. Get a journal and write what you feel the Lord says to you.

(The first thought you have, that does not go against anything the Bible teaches, is usually God. The second thought usually is us doubting and talking ourselves out of what God just spoke to us.)

---

[27] "Cedrus Libani." Wikipedia. Accessed August 17, 2016. https://en.wikipedia.org/wiki/Cedrus_libani.

[28] Burwell, By Gerald. "Editor's Note – Storytelling - VIE Magazine." VIE Magazine. 2010. Accessed October 04, 2016. http://viemagazine.com/article/editors-note-storytelling/.

# twenty-one

## DEMONSTRATING VICTORY

Demonstrate
verb (used with object), demonstrated, demonstrating.
1. to make evident or establish by arguments or reasoning;
prove:
to demonstrate a philosophical principle.
2.to describe, explain, or illustrate by examples,
specimens, experiments, or the like: to demonstrate the
force of gravity by dropping an object.
3.to manifest or exhibit; show:
He demonstrated his courage by his actions in battle.
4.to display openly or publicly, as feelings:
to demonstrate one's anger by slamming a door.[29]

Demonstrate means to manifest, prove and publicly display something. We can't just talk about victory, we have to publicly display it. If God is calling us to walk in his victory, what does it look like? We can't display something if we don't know what it looks like. We must understand what we are to demonstrate. The greatest example of that is Jesus. To demonstrate it we must look like it, talk like it, act like it, and be like it.

## (ACT LIKE IT) CULTURE OF KINDNESS

Kindness may be thought of as a good, simple thing. It's not just a simple thing, it's a transformational thing. Kindness has the ability to open the hardest of hearts and touch us at our core. It has the ability to make people come alive. Kindness is the expression of God's heart towards us. When we show kindness to others, we are sharing God's heart.

> Instead, be kind to each other, tenderhearted, forgiving one another, just as God through Christ has forgiven you. (Ephesians 4:32 NLT)

This is one of multiple scriptures where God tells us to be kind. The fact that God tells us that we need to be kind lets me know that kindness is not instinctual. It lets me know that it is something I have to chose to do intentionally. Kindness is from God and is God's nature. He is asking us to represent his nature. He wants us to express kindness to people around us because it shows the kindness that God has to give us. We have to express and demonstrate what we have received. The more we express that kindness, the easier it will become to show that kindness again. We are demonstrating God's heart to people.

We must also make sure we are showing kindness to the people closest to us. We need to show kindness to our spouses, our kids, our family, our friends, and our co-workers. As we show kindness to them, we create an atmosphere and a culture of kindness. The more we are kind, the more people will be kind to us. Have you noticed when you meet someone kind, it makes you want to be extra kind back to them? Kindness produces kindness.

It is always great to show kindness to others. There is one person most of us always overlook when showing kindness. That person is ourselves. Sometimes it can be easier to show kindness to others, more than to ourselves. We must also be kind to ourselves. When we make a mistake, we need to forgive ourselves quickly.

Expressing kindness continually will not only change others, it will also change you. As we are kind it brings healing to our hearts, because we have to soften our hearts to be kind. It causes us to open our hearts and look beyond ourselves. Through this, we are releasing God's victory.

Create an atmosphere around you that is kind. Speak kind words. Treat yourself and others kindly.

## (LOOK LIKE IT) JOY AND PEACE

> for the kingdom of God is not eating and drinking, but righteousness and peace and joy in the Holy Spirit. For he who in this way serves Christ is acceptable to God and approved by men. (Romans 14:17-18 NASB)

We are called to not live by this world's standard of pleasure and satisfaction. We are called to live in the kingdom of God's standard. The way of the kingdom is pleasure in righteousness, peace and joy produced by the Holy Spirit. When people see us, they should see the victory of God on us. We should look like we have joy and peace. We should not be walking around sad and depressed. Don't look like your family is being held hostage by a band of ninjas, and you are desperate for money to get karate lessons to rescue them. If you are a member of a championship team, you walk around confident in your team's ability to win. We are a part of God's team. We must rest in the fact that our team wins; God is victorious.

We must live lives demonstrating righteousness, peace and joy. Through that, we will please God and others will approve of us. What does it mean that others would approve us? It means they think favorably of us. That means they are more likely to desire to be around you. People desire to be around a victorious person. It's exciting to be around someone full of life and energy. It's great to be around someone who lights up a room and brings joy. No one wants to not have joy. As people of victory, we should be bringing the joy and peace of God wherever we go. People should want us around. Your community should want you around. We should be making a difference wherever we are. Victory is having joy and peace. We should have it and it should be desirable to others. Our lives should be lead by the Holy Spirit.

## (BE LIKE IT) VICTORY IN HARD TIMES

> And we know [with great confidence] that God [who is deeply concerned about us] causes all things to work together [as a plan] for good for those who love God, to

those who are called according to His plan and purpose.
(Romans 8:28 AMP)

You can still have hope in the middle of living in this world, this world that can be hard, harsh, lonely, disappointing and sad. This is a fact: hard things happen here on earth where we live. Yes, it gets hard sometimes for everyone.

To be in victory does not mean everything is perfect. It does mean that we are settled in our hearts that we know God is working all things out for our good. That means when things are hard, we can trust that God is still with us. This is not a quote on a nice card. This is the word of God. It comes with the same authority that spoke the world into existence in Genesis. God is always at work for our good.

We must have a Heavenly mindset. A Heavenly mindset can see through the hard situation and see God working in the middle of it. If we focus on all the earthly things, that will leave us discouraged and hopeless. Whatever we face in this life, God is on our side. He is out to help us through. We have to have our eyes on the Lord and focus our gaze on him. As we look at him, he will strengthen us. When we believe God is working for our good, we are walking in victory.

## (TALK LIKE IIT) MIRACLES

As Jesus was walking along, he saw a man who had been blind from birth. "Rabbi," his disciples asked him, "why was this man born blind? Was it because of his own sins or his parents' sins?" "It was not because of his sins or his parents' sins," Jesus answered. "This happened so the power of God could be seen in him. We must quickly carry out the tasks assigned us by the one who sent us.[a] The night is coming, and then no one can work. But while I am here in the world, I am the light of the world." Then he spit on the ground, made mud with the saliva, and spread the mud over the blind man's eyes. He told him, "Go wash yourself in the pool of Siloam" (Siloam means "sent"). So the man went and washed and came back seeing!" John 9:1-7 (NTL)

Miracles are a great demonstration of victory. To pray for the physical issue and see God heal it is such a tangible demonstration. It is God's victory being seen. We see in the scripture above that the disciples wanted to focus on why this man was born blind. Jesus was like, "Well that's not what I want to focus on." What caused the problem does not matter as much as what Jesus wants to do about the problem. He said this was going to bring glory to God. God healed the man's blindness.

This man and everyone that knew him saw that he got a miracle from God. The power of God was displayed. This man who was blind since birth now had the ability to see. God touched this man and changed his life. This miracle was the victory of God. It was God bringing his victory over this man's blindness. Every time God heals someone, that's his victory on display.

God wants to use us to pray for the sick and watch them be healed. He wants to display his victory through us to impact the world around us with his power. You are a connection point that God has to release his victory into this world. Jesus was the first example of that displayed throughout the New Testament. God wants miracles to flow through you.

## THREE EASY STEPS TO SEE MIRACLES

1. Believe that God wants to use you. By the way, if you did not know that, now you do. He wants to use you. Don't make that face with me. He does.
2. Pray for the sick. Go find a sick person and pray for them.
3. Expect the miracle, and ask them to do what they could not do before.

I am not talking to you from something I have not done. I have done and seen this many times. I have seen deaf ears open, broken bones healed, and pain immediately leave people. The victory of healing is real, and God wants to use you to do it. I don't mean to over simplify it... wait, actually I do. We have made so many rules out of our experiences that we don't even try anymore. Try. Step out and do it.

If you need a physical miracle right now, receive healing as I pray for you.

> Lord, I ask you to release your victory in this reader's body through your healing power right now. Pain Go. Chemical and hormonal levels balance out now. Tight muscles be loosed. Growth dissipate now. Bones be restored. Body be made whole. In Jesus Name!

---

[29] "Demonstrate." Dictionary.com. Accessed July 10, 2016. http://www.dictionary.com/browse/demonstrate.

# twenty-two

## YOUR VALUE

How do you know the value of something? In economics, the value of something boils down to what people are willing to pay for that thing. The value is based on what it's worth to you. If you are at a local store, you might be willing to only pay $1 for a bottle of water. Is a bottle of water at a theme park worth $10? If you're thirsty enough, it is. If you are in the desert and have not had water in 24 hours, you might be willing to spend $1000 on that same bottle of water. Did that bottle of water change? No, but your level of desire for the bottle of water did.

I believe that principle about finding the value of something is true for us also. How much is someone willing to spend on us? God was wiling to spend the life of his own son to buy us. There is no greater value than that: you and I cost the life of someone. Someone was killed for my value. That may sound harsh. God looked around Heaven and said, "What is the most valuable thing I can give? I want them to understand their own value to me." God was willing to sacrifice his most precious, most valuable item for us. God let his son be killed for us. John 15:13 (NKJV) says that greater love has no one than this: to lay down one's life for one's friends. God laid down his life for you. You are worth dying for. God loves you!

> And they sang a new song, saying: "You are worthy to take the scroll and to open its seals, because you were slain, and with your blood you purchased for God persons from every tribe and language and people and nation." (Revelation. 5:9 NIV)

111

Jesus paid a high price to buy us. He paid for us with his blood. We don't own ourselves. We are owned by God. Once you buy something, it no longer belongs to the store anymore. You own it. We belong to Jesus. We belong to the kindest, most compassionate, loving, caring, passionate being in all existence. We belong to God. Talk about a confidence boost. If we can let this drop down into our hearts, our self-value will go through the roof.

We were purchased by victory from defeat. We are owned by victory. So whenever defeat tries to operate in our lives, we need to tell it, "You don't own me." We belong to victory. We have to learn to rest and trust in this fact. We should adopt the mindset of the one who owns us. We should adopt his mindset of victory. I understand it's not always easy to feel this way everyday. We must fight for this to be the dominating belief in our hearts and minds. We must do what 2 Corinthians 10:5 says:

> casting down arguments and every high thing that exalts itself against the knowledge of God, bringing every thought into captivity to the obedience of Christ... (NKJV)

We must reject every thought that tries to put itself above how God feels about us. We were purchased with a high price. We were bought with blood. Everything that says we are not valuable is a lie. There is no higher amount you can pay for something than with your own life. We are expensive. We are the best of the best product. We are worth more than anything you can think of. Our value comes from God, nothing else.

# twenty-three

## DEPENDANCE ON JESUS

…and the boat were already a considerable distance from land, buffeted by the waves because the wind was against it. Shortly before dawn, Jesus went out to them, walking on the lake. When the disciples saw him walking on the lake, they were terrified. "It's a ghost," they said and cried out in fear. But Jesus immediately said to them: "Take courage! It is I. Don't be afraid." "Lord, if it's you," Peter replied, "tell me to come to you on the water." "Come," he said. Then Peter got down out of the boat, walked on the water and came toward Jesus. But when he saw the wind, he was afraid and, beginning to sink, cried out, "Lord, save me!" Immediately Jesus reached out his hand and caught him. "You of little faith," he said, "why did you doubt?" And when they climbed into the boat, the wind died down. (Matthew 14:24-32 NIV)

Peter said to Jesus, "If it's you tell me to come on the water." Peter desired to be with Jesus. I am sure Peter was not thinking about walking on water. Peter desired the Lord enough to leave the dry, comfortable boat for Jesus. Jesus said "Yes, you can come." Peter trusted Jesus and went to him. Peter got into trouble when he took his eyes off of Jesus. He forgot about the one he desired and began to see himself doing something that was impossible. He started seeing the wind and waves around him. They were telling him "You can't do this." He began to believe those things and began to sink. Peter's ability to walk on the water was tied to Jesus. When we are dependent upon Jesus, we can walk in victory.

Our ability to live in victory is tied only to him. He is victory, and he shares his victory with us. The moment we think we can produce victory in ourselves, we will see quickly how wrong we are. We depend on his ability to see victory in our lives.

## VICTORY IS YOURS

> If any of you lacks wisdom, let him ask of God, who gives to all liberally and without reproach, and it will be given to him. But let him ask in faith, with no doubting, for he who doubts is like a wave of the sea driven and tossed by the wind. For let not that man suppose that he will receive anything from the Lord; he is a double-minded man, unstable in all his ways. (James 1:5-8 NKJV)

We have to be convinced that victory is ours, and it's not about our worthiness but about his. We have to not be schizophrenic in our thinking. If we ask for God to show his victory in our lives, we must believe that he will do it. God wants to release his victory to you and through you. For years the the religious system has yelled loudly that God is angry with you and is against you. I want to break that lie off of you. God is not mad at you. He is seeking a way to you. He sent Jesus to build the bridge from his heart to your heart.

We have victory because he is victorious. He is seeking to share his victory with us. We get to experience his victory when we are connected to him. We lean on him to receive it. We must be like Peter and say "I want to step out of where I am and step into the place where you are because I desire you."

As we step out, we will see his victory released in our lives, without excessive effort. The reason is that his world is victory. When we step into his world, we can then begin to experience it. Every problem will not disappear. Yet you will have the ability to walk through it in such a way as to defy the rules of how it will affect you. God will give us the ability to see and do things that are beyond our abilities.

# VICTORY BY COVENANT

> This is my blood of the covenant, which is poured out for
> many for the forgiveness of sins. (Matthew 26:28 NIV)

We are in victory because we are in covenant with God. He shed his blood to bring us into covenant with him. Covenants are made between two parties. Each is required to meet certain standards for the covenant. Jesus fulfilled 99.9% of the covenant. Our .1% is just to believe what he has said. In ancient times, once you entered into a covenant, you were tied to that person for life. There was no separation between you and that person. What benefited them benefited you. What hurt them hurt you. The entire Bible is a covenant between God and us. He has tied himself to us forever. He has invited us to partake of his divine ways of victory.

God made a covenant with us, but not because we have anything to offer him. God covenanted with us because he loves us and loves to share with us. God wants to bring victory into our lives. God's victory transforms us. God shares his victory with us in our weakness. Victory is knowing him, walking with him and loving him.

# twenty-four

## THE PERSON OF VICTORY

Throughout this book, we have talked about victory. I have given you examples of victory. I have demonstrated the concept of victory. This is the crescendo. I want to introduce you to victory. It's not a concept, not an ideal, not a goal, not a state of mind, not a feeling, and not a principle. Victory is a person. Jesus is Victory. Hey friend, meet the man, the legend himself. This is the crown jewel of Heaven. This is the one whom it's all about.

### JESUS CHRIST!

Isaiah 6:1 tells us that he wears victory as a garment. Let's think about things owned by someone influential. I had the opportunity to sit in the Rolls-Royce Phantom III that Sir Winston Churchill and General Dwight D. Eisenhower discussed the plans for D-day in. And it was on the 71st anniversary of D-day. It was awesome. There really was nothing special about the car. The car only has value and significance because of who owned it. The robe of victory we see the Lord wearing in Isaiah 6:1(NKJV) is only important and valuable because the Lord is wearing it. The mantle of victory he is wearing speaks of him. This mantle is only an expression of him. The mantle has lesser value than him. If he wears a mantle of victory, then how much more victorious is he? If Isaiah was impressed by his mantle, how much more impressive is he?

Jesus is the full embodiment of victory; the prize we are reaching for.; the answer to every defeat in our lives. He is the trophy of victory.

He is the answer to every pain, to every struggle, to every fear, to every worry, to every anxiety.

Usually treasure is kept locked up, surrounded by armed guards and protection. It is kept out of reach of the masses. However, Jesus is the most unique of all treasures. He comes running full-force with arms wide open to us, completely touchable and reachable, saying "I am here for you. I have come to rescue you from defeat." He needs no protection. He is not fragile, weak or incapable. He is mighty, powerful, strong, bold and courageous. He is not a fairytale. He is the real deal.

## JESUS CONQUERED HELL AND DEATH

He, foreseeing this, spoke concerning the resurrection of the Christ, that His soul was not left in Hades, nor did His flesh see corruption. (Acts 2:31NKJV)

Therefore He says: "When He ascended on high, He led captivity captive, And gave gifts to men."[a] (Now this, "He ascended"—what does it mean but that He also first[b] descended into the lower parts of the earth? He who descended is also the One who ascended far above all the heavens, that He might fill all things.) (Ephesians 4:8-12 NKJV)

I am the Living One; I was dead, and now look, I am alive for ever and ever! And I hold the keys of death and Hades. (Revelation 1:18 NIV)

Jesus conquered hell and death. Jesus went into hell and left leading captivity captive. He imprisoned the thing that was imprisoning. He put a limitation on the thing that was defeating every person. He stopped the consuming force of defeat by stepping into the middle of it and defeating it. He is victory. Victory operates the same way light does. In a dark room, you flip the switch and light comes on. Darkness does not argue; it responds immediately by submitting to light. When victory shows up, defeat submits. Jesus brought victory over defeat itself. Victory showed up and defeat had to bow its knee.

## JESUS CONQUERED THE DEVIL

> And again: "I will put My trust in Him."And again: "Here am I and the children whom God has given Me." Inasmuch then as the children have partaken of flesh and blood, He Himself likewise shared in the same, that through death He might destroy him who had the power of death, that is, the devil, and release those who through fear of death were all their lifetime subject to bondage. (Hebrews 2:13-15 NKJV)

> And having disarmed the powers and authorities, he made a public spectacle of them, triumphing over them by the cross. Colossians 2:15 (NIV)

> None of the rulers of this age understood it, for if they had, they would not have crucified the Lord of glory. 1 Corinthians 2:8 (NIV)

Jesus destroyed the Devil. We see in Hebrews 2:13-15 (NASB) that Jesus takes responsibility for us. Before we chose him, he chose us. He fought to set us free from a lifetime subjected to bondage. Let me take some pressure off of you. Before we even knew we needed freedom, he chose to set us free because of who he is, not because of who we are. God is not sitting in Heaven looking for ways to punish us. He is looking for ways to free us. He is very passionate about us living lives of victory. When we live lives of victory, we reflect him.

God is fighting for you. He feels responsible for you. He is protecting you. Jesus intended that through death, he would destroy the power of the Devil over you. Jesus went into the enemy's territory and defeated him. He defeated the Devil where the Devil had home-court advantage. That is a display of victory.

We see in Colossians 2:15 (NASB) the level at which Jesus conquered the enemy. He made a public spectacle of triumphing over the enemy at the cross. In ancient Roman times, when their military commanders returned from a foreign war with a significant victory, they would have an event called Roman triumph:

> The Roman triumph (triumphus) was a civil ceremony and religious rite of ancient Rome, held to publicly celebrate and sanctify the success of a military commander who had led Roman forces to victory in the service of the state or, originally and traditionally, one who had successfully completed a foreign war.
>
> On the day of his triumph, the general wore a crown of laurel and the all-purple, gold-embroidered triumphal toga picta ("painted" toga), regalia that identified him as near-divine or near-kingly, and even was known to paint his face red. He rode in a four-horse chariot through the streets of Rome in unarmed procession with his army, captives, and the spoils of his war.[30]

This paints the picture of Jesus' triumph. Jesus defeated the enemy and then led a parade showing the defeat of the enemy to all. The enemy could not even estimate the level of triumph Jesus what about to display through the cross. The scripture said they would not have crucified him if they knew.

## ACCESS TO VICTORY

The cross declares that we have access to victory. Victory is hope, joy, life, peace, healing, love, kindness, gentleness, patience, long-suffering, laughter, grace, mercy, and so much more. The cross declares we can have victory in our lives every day. As Jesus was on the cross, I believe he was looking at each one of us and saying "I am giving you access to my victory." He was giving us access to himself. Two thousand years ago Jesus purchased our victory. It's now ours to receive. He broke through, and we must follow behind him into it. It's like birds flying in a V formation. The bird at the head of the V exerts the most energy. He has to push against the wind resistance. The birds flying behind ride on the airflow created by the head bird, just outside the wingtip of the previous bird. They get an easier flight. This helps all the birds be able to fly faster and further than they could on their own. We must stay close behind Jesus. This is our new home. We must vacate the place of defeat and move into his victory, found under the shadow of his wings.

Victory is not an action or outward state. It's our position in Jesus. No matter what is going on around you, you can still be in a state of victory if you have embraced and received the victorious one, Jesus Christ.

The enemy has no comparison to us. He is defeat. The only card he has to play is convincing us to take his defeat. It's like starting a race when you're already at the finish line, while your opponent is at the start. There's no competition.

## RELEASE VICTORY WHEREVER YOU GO

We now live from a position of victory. We are not fighting for victory, we are fighting from victory. We are enforcing that victory in our minds, bodies, lives, families, houses, churches, communities and nations. We release God's victory into every place he has called us:

> These signs will accompany those who have believed: in My name they will cast out demons, they will speak with new tongues; they will pick up serpents, and if they drink any deadly poison, it will not hurt them; they will lay hands on the sick, and they will recover. (Mark 16:17-18 NASB)

This sounds like us releasing his victory to me. We demonstrate him. We bring forth his victory. Every time his victory is displayed, he gets glory. Walking in victory gives glory to God. When you are walking in victory, you are agreeing with God and valuing what he has done. Every time you overcome, it says "God is with me, because I can't overcome in my own strength." When you let defeat rule you, you're saying, "God, what you did was not enough for me to overcome." Let's give God the glory he deserves. His shed blood was enough to free me from defeat. What he did worked. I just have to believe it.

When defeat tries to speak to you, declare "I am victorious, because Jesus won me access to his victory." To become the person of victory is to let go of who you think you are. It is actively stepping into who Jesus says that you are. Victory is believing your God-given identity.

God's victory is not just to be displayed within the church. God's victory is to be released into the world. Wherever you are, whatever you do, release victory. Let the person of victory be displayed. Don't let defeat keep you and the person of victory bound from operating in open display.

You no longer have to settle for defeat. Victory has been made possible. Jesus is our victory. The lie has been shattered. You have victory in Jesus, and every lie of defeat must be silent. Your heart must believe victory is yours, then you will not tolerate the enemy's ways of defeat. Declare your victory every day. You walk with the person of victory, Jesus Christ.

---

[30] "Roman Triumph." Wikipedia. Accessed August 25, 2016. https://en.wikipedia.org/wiki/Roman_triumph.

# twenty-five

## VICTORIOUS MENTALITY

Jesus paid a high price to bring us into a life of victory. He gave his life to reposition ours. We have to shift our mindset to live that way. When someone becomes a police officer, his or her mindset changes. This person don't walk around acting like a regular citizen. While wearing that uniform, this person represents something bigger than him or herself. Now this person acts like a person in authority. The officer looks at any situation with the knowledge that he or she brings order and safety. This person now has authority.

> au·thor·i·ty
> 1. the power to determine, adjudicate, or otherwise settle issues or disputes; jurisdiction; the right to control, command, or determine.
> 2. a power or right delegated or given; authorization: Who has the authority to grant permission?
> 3. a person or body of persons in whom authority is vested, as a governmental agency.
> 4. Usually, authorities. persons having the legal power to make and enforce the law; government: They finally persuaded the authorities that they were not involved in espionage.
> 5. an accepted source of information, advice, etc.[31]

To have authority means to have the power to enforce laws and settle issues. When we give our lives to Jesus, we gain authority under his leadership. We have to see ourselves with that authority. He has given us the power to enforce his laws here on earth. This authority was given to us at the very beginning. The enemy tried to take that authority from us. Jesus won it back from the enemy and gave it back to us.

> Then God said, "Let Us make man in Our image, according to Our likeness; and let them rule over the fish of the sea and over the birds of the sky and over the cattle and over all the earth, and over every creeping thing that creeps on the earth." (Genesis 1:26 NASB)
> Do·min·ion
> 1. the power or right of governing and controlling; sovereign authority.
> 2. rule; control; domination.
> 3. a territory, usually of considerable size, in which a single rulership holds sway.
> 4. lands or domains subject to sovereignty or control.
> 5. Government . a territory constituting a self-governing commonwealth and being one of a number of such territories united in a community of nations, or empire: formerly applied to self-governing divisions of the British Empire, as Canada and New Zealand.[32]

We see in Genesis 1:26 (NASB) that God gave us dominion over the things of the earth. God has given us the governing right in the earth. We have been given that right by God to manage his will and purpose. We are not given this to showoff our power or dominance. We are given this to show forth his power and victory.

The enemy has used the same trick since Genesis. He tried to convince Adam that he was not like God. Adam believed that lie and ate the fruit. He thought this would make him like God. What Adam did not realize was that he was already like God. He was created in God's image and likeness. The enemy was able to get power when he convinced Adam to give up his power. The only authority the enemy has is what we have given him.

## AUTHORITY TO OVERCOME THE DEVIL

> for everyone born of God overcomes the world. This is
> the victory that has overcome the world, even our faith.
> (1 John 5:4 NIV)

> … The reason the Son of God appeared was to destroy
> the devil's work. (1 John 3:8 NIV)

We overcome the things of the world by being in right order under the authority of God. He leads; our authority is from submitting under his authority. When Jesus ascended to Heaven, that job did not end. We are to continue to destroy the works of the devil. Jesus placed the authority in our hands. We have been authorized to continue this.

> The breaker is come up before them: they have broken
> up, and have passed through the gate, and are gone out
> by it: and their king shall pass before them, and the Lord
> on the head of them. (Micah 2:13 KJV)

Jesus Christ is the breaker. We must follow behind him to advance. He leads us to have victory over the enemy. Without the Lord, their is no victory. He is Victory! In the Old Testament they would not go into battle unless the Lord was with them. They knew they could not go into battle without the person of victory present. He was their victory. He is also our victory.

## TAKE AUTHORITY IN OUR MINDS

> We demolish arguments and every pretension that sets
> itself up against the knowledge of God, and we take
> captive every thought to make it obedient to Christ. (2
> Corinthians 10:5 NIV)

The first platform we have to take authority over is our mind. We must not let the enemy run free in our minds. We can't let our thoughts run with lies from the enemy. We must rule our thoughts. We must evict the enemy from living in our minds. We can't allow thoughts of fear, failure, defeat and inferiority to rule. We must let victory rule in our minds.

Every thought that is against what God says about us must be pushed out. We have limited real estate in our minds. We should not let the enemy fill it up. We should let God fill it with his ways. Our minds were created by God as a tool to help facilitate his victory. We can't let this God-given tool be used by the enemy. Destroy the thoughts that desire to fight against God and his ways. Let God have the most actionable real estate in your mind. If you can defeat the enemy here, you can bring external victory wherever you go.

Pray this prayer: *Lord I submit to your authority over my life. I submit my mind to you. I ask you to uproot every thought in my mind that is in direct opposition to you. I ask you to plant your thoughts in my mind. Lord teach me how to live from a mindset of victory. In Jesus Name.*

Read scripture daily to build God's thoughts in your mind.

## TAKE AUTHORITY FOR THOSE AROUND US

> Be devoted to one another in love. Honor one another
> above yourselves. (Romans 12:10 NIV)

We don't have authority to dominate people. We have authority to serve people. We serve them by exercising our authority against the enemy to benefit them. We can serve them into life and freedom. God has brought us into freedom. Our freedom and victory are not just for ourselves. It is to be released to others. God wants us to serve others. We should be the kindest people around. We should be the first ones to reach out and help. We should be first to give, volunteer and care for others.

We have the person of victory living inside of us. We should let him impact the people we come in contact with daily. What we have is powerful and can make a difference. What we have is real. We must push past the intimidation of the enemy and demonstrate what we have. If someone needs healing in his or her body, pray for that person. God wants to use you more than you realize. He is passionate to use you.

We can impact every person we come in contact with. It does not have to be this big, long thing: share a kind word, smile or tell a funny story. Every interaction can release God's victory. Through a simple act you can lessen the defeat in someone's life.

## TAKE AUTHORITY ON THE JOB

> Work willingly at whatever you do, as though you were
> working for the Lord rather than for people. (Colossians
> 3:2 NLT)

We must work in whatever we do as though God hired us, because he did. Wether you work at a fast food place or are CEO of a Fortune 500 company, you do it unto the Lord. Our work is a tool in how we serve God. This verse is instructions from God of how we are to approach work. We don't just do it to get money. We must do it like someone we love has asked us to do them a favor. We do it with our whole heart. We must not do the bear minimum, but give all that we can.

When we give our best and do our best, we create an opportunity for God to shine. When we shine, people will take notice. Our willingness to work hard shows a heart to serve. A heart to serve demonstrates God's heart. People will take notice of that. You can bring victory to your job by being an employee that brings great value to that place.

> "Do not muzzle an ox while it is treading out the
> grain,"and "The worker deserves his wages." (1 Timothy
> 5:18 NIV)

If you work hard and do a good job, people will pay you well. Work hard, be the best and rise to the top. Having the heart to serve will give you the influence to bring change and impact. You can change the atmosphere on your job. You become the standard by which all work is measured when you work with a heart unto God.

# TAKE AUTHORITY IN YOUR REGION

We can bring victory to our region. We have a voice in our communities. For a long time, the church has functioned in a run-and-hide mentality. As we ran and hid, the enemy came and took areas that we left unoccupied. We have run to our homes and church buildings. As we did, the world became a darker place. The main reason is the that light went and hid under a bushel.

We must let our God-given victory shine brightly. We must stand up against injustice in our communities. Believers should be at local government meetings. We need to hear what issues our communities face. We can pray for these issues, and then we can move into action to serve our region to bring change. We can fight against unjust laws. We can stand up for what is right. If we don't speak up, of coarse the enemy will. We are the ones with the most just and righteous code by which to live. The world cannot teach us how to live and operate righteously in society. We must lead society in the ways of God.

# LET GOD ARISE

Let God arise, Let His enemies be scattered;
Let those also who hate Him flee before Him.
(Psalm 68:1 NKJV)

Arise means "to stand, establish."[33] Scattered means to "dash in pieces or break."[34] Let God arise where you are. Let him set the standard of how things are to be. If you let God arise, he will break the darkness that is present. It's like the story in 1 Samuel 5:4 (NKJV). They had the ark of the covenant in the temple of a false god. Then the next morning when they went into the temple, the statue of the false god was knocked over. When God arises, he will bring down the false gods.

The true church of God in this day will arise with power and have authority over darkness. We will see the enemies of God scattered. It is a time of God causing his church to arise in his victory. A victorious church is arising.

Victory is a choice. We must choose it. We don't just get victory. We get what we choose. We must continually choose victory in every moment. Let God bring forth victory through you in your everyday life. We can be the light of victory to the world around us. Our relationship with defeat is over! Let our eternal relationship with victory begin today!

Make this declaration:

> *Defeat, I break up with you. I breakup with you in my mind, in my actions, in my emotions, and in all areas of my life. I choose to accept and receive the victory that Jesus purchased for me. I am victorious! I have victory in every area of my life! My victory is not based on my outward situations, it is based on my internal positioning with Jesus. I am victorious!*

---

[31] "Authority." Dictionary.com. Accessed July 10, 2016. http://www.dictionary.com/browse/authority?s=t.

[32] "Dominion." Dictionary.com. Accessed July 10, 2016. http://www.dictionary.com/browse/dominion.

[33] "Strong's H6965." Blue Letter Bible. Accessed January 10, 2017. https://www.blueletterbible.org/lang/Lexicon/Lexicon.cfm?strongs=H6965&t=KJV.

[34] "Strong's H6327." Blue Letter Bible. Accessed January 10, 2017. https://www.blueletterbible.org/lang/Lexicon/Lexicon.cfm?strongs=H6327&t=KJV.

# Scriptures of Victory

1 Chronicles 29:11 (NIV)
Yours, LORD, is the greatness and the power and the glory and the majesty and the splendor, for everything in heaven and earth is yours. Yours, LORD, is the kingdom; you are exalted as head over all.

Psalm 98:1 (NLT)
A psalm. Sing a new song to the LORD, for he has done wonderful deeds. His right hand has won a mighty victory; his holy arm has shown his saving power!

Psalm 47:1 (NKJV)
Oh, clap your hands, all you peoples! Shout to God with the voice of triumph!

Psalm 47:5 (NKJV)
God has gone up with a shout, The Lord with the sound of a trumpet.

Isaiah 25:8 (NLT)
He will swallow up death forever! The Sovereign LORD will wipe away all tears. He will remove forever all insults and mockery against his land and people. The LORD has spoken!

Psalms 91:7 (NIV)
A thousand may fall at your side, ten thousand at your right hand, but it will not come near you.

Matthew 12:20 (NIV)

A bruised reed he will not break, and a smoldering wick he will not snuff out, till he has brought justice through to victory.

1 Corinthians 15:54 (NLT)

Then, when our dying bodies have been transformed into bodies that will never die, this Scripture will be fulfilled: "Death is swallowed up in victory.

1 Corinthians 15:57 (NLT)

But thank God! He gives us victory over sin and death through our Lord Jesus Christ.

Isaiah 42:13 (NIV)

The LORD will march out like a champion, like a warrior he will stir up his zeal; with a shout he will raise the battle cry and will triumph over his enemies.

Hey guys, I hope you enjoyed this book and it released victory into your heart. Stay connected with me on social media. Share testimonies of the victories that you are now walking in. Use the hashtag #BREAKUPWITHDEFEAT and follow us on Instagram @kingjermaine. I would love to see us create a culture of victory. I want to hear your victory story.

# About the Author

Jermaine Francis has been active in ministry for over 10 years. He and his wife travel nationally and internationally, speaking at conferences, schools, and churches. He has a passion to see believers find, embrace, and release their unique God given destiny and use it to impact the world for Jesus.

Jermaine felt a call to ministry in High School and began to answer that call by serving in the youth group. He attended Valor Christian College in Columbus, OH under Pastor Rod Parsley. Later received his Bachelor's degree from Christian International School of Theology.

Jermaine and his wife live in Santa Rosa Beach, FL where they are on staff at Christian International Ministries founded by Dr. Bill Hamon.